I0437700

# The Return of the Kings

Thomas Purcell

Copyright © 2011 Thomas Purcell
All rights reserved.
ISBN-13: **978-1460977033**

# DEDICATION

To Mom and Dad

Whose faith and belief in me never wavered

and

to


Annie

Without whom this book could not have been possible.

# CONTENTS

# Preface

*There is nothing new except what has been forgotten.*
*-Marie                    Antoinette*

For those of you who may not have noticed, a number of world leaders have been attending environmental theory meetings with a lot of enthusiasm and public speeches in the last few years. And why? They are representative of the turn of the tides of power away from the freedom of capitalism and a return to the tyranny of the elite over the individual. What is the motivating force behind the move away from capitalism? A political force known as the "Green Movement" is attempting to return control of resources back once again to government in the form of a planned economy . In short, it is a restoration of the forces of feudalism.

Excuse me, what? Feudalism?

In the "bad old days" of the Middle Ages government was primarily run by a concept described by some historians as feudalism. Although many simply describe feudalism as despotic rule and/or tyranny,

—

5

feudalism is a term used when the elite or nobility has control over lower classes and their resources through voluntary or deeded titular title and landholdings.

So how does that relate to environmentalism, global warming and the Green movement?

The nobility in those days kept tight control over the kingdom's resources. Shooting a king's deer or mining or drilling for water on the king's land meant severe repercussions for those doing so without permission from the king. Permission was defined as a title and for that title, a certain tax or "levy" was assessed yearly by the king. Thus control of those resources allowed the king to maintain power through the use of those tax funds to amass armies and defend their noble rights. The taxation levels in many cases were quite onerous, sapping the economic productivity of the citizens. It also made it difficult for the citizenry to amount to much during a civil insurrection since they could not raise capital to amass weapons without significant resource holdings. Using this system, nobles held sway over large portions of the world for many generations.

It was not until the rise of mechanization, the ability of the masses to gather wealth, and the eventual expansion into the New World, that this system finally lost its grip over mankind. Keep in mind, this was fairly recent from an historical point of view--only about 350 years. The control of the kingdom's resources goes back to the Roman Empire, and the concept of classes and nobility even further.

Now look at the Green Movement. What does it want to accomplish? Firstly, it wants the people of the world to stop using up resources and issue harsh penalties to those that do not comply. Greens want to control the distribution of resources, limit those who control their respective governments and to essentially centrally control the distribution of said resources (i.e. wealth) to the citizens either by birth or status. This form of government social justice is seen in America's push for economic reform under the guise of cap and trade rules for example. The wealthy or "nobles" will be able to buy carbon credits to use as much resources as they want, while the poorer people will have to limit their consumption.

Sound familiar?

One of the big shakers and movers in this movement is guess who--the Royal House of Windsor and Prince Charles. Charles has been highly supportive on the environmental movement for some time and heavily involved in the green efforts worldwide. It would benefit the royal houses greatly for a return to centralized resource control and thus centralized power in the hands of the few. Most of the other royal houses of Europe are also similarly aligned with Charles on this matter, as well as the current President of the United States, Barack Obama.

Keep in mind that it does not take all these leaders to actively conspire together to restore power. They act in a similar fashion to achieve a common goal--power and wealth in the hands of the few, with control over the hands of the many. It is not a conspiracy theory to say that many people are working toward the same end.

The big culprit and enemy in this Green Movement is the American people and business interests who for years have amassed power and wealth in their free citizenry by thumbing their noses at the nobility, killing as many of the king's deer as they could and establishing the first true free republic in human history under the banner of capitalism. I am sure more than a few blue bloods are a wee bit upset that 1,500 years of power and rule came to a screeching stop.

And now we have a President who fell for the green story, hook line and sinker. The President believes, like most of Europe and some of Asia, that America is somehow evil for making the most of her vast natural resources and allowing individuals to have the highest standard of living in the world while limiting the power of its leaders. Shameful aren't we? Shameful that America produces 90% of the world's wealth without so much as a good whipping or a month in the dungeon to build character.

That is what these geniuses will send us back to if they have their way. Exploding our debt while increasing our energy costs and limiting personal wealth and limiting personal freedoms will certainly go a long way to keeping the American people in line though--won't it?

In this book, the premise that European nobility has been expanding its interests in the Green Movement will be examined and explored. It will point out the enormous powers that are involved in the attempt to destroy capitalism and how the Royal houses of Europe are the primary financial driving force behind the movement.

Bah--down with the Kings! Long live American capitalism and the freedoms it brings.

# The Royals

*"Necessity is the plea for every infringement of human freedom. It is the argument of tyrants; it is the creed of slaves."* -William Pitt

The world is a changing place, ever evolving from our pre-technology Stone Age roots, to a modern day enlightened culture. That process not only includes our evolution as a species through the means of technology but also through our sociological and political development. It is in this way that human beings become more civilized and advanced, and society becomes more comfortable via a better standard of living. Society learns from mistakes as well as successes, and in the end, hopefully, mankind improves. Human beings have progressed more in the past 500 years than they did in the past 5,000, and with such quick development our wisdom often finds it difficult to keep up.

Since the earliest civilizations people around the world have strained to resolve the old issue of protecting the environment versus the practical application of industry and growth. It is the nature of manufacturing and industry that environmental conditions suffer as a result of its expansion. Pollutants are emitted, and those pollutants can be hazardous to the long-term health of the individual or the environment. Even as early as the Roman imperial period, the subject of environmental concerns was evident in their writings. Roman Emperor Justinian wrote that water and air were public property for the benefit of all,[1] and over the years the Romans spent enormous sums on the age old problems of clean water and garbage disposal.[2] Some of the earliest cultures had this same problem. Archaeologists have found that even in the oldest cultures the issue of waste disposal and protecting the primary living area sanitarily and efficiently was a key motivator in the shape and design of habitations.

Today these concepts of environmentalism, government protectionism and a planned society are

---

[1] *In Law We Trust -- Can environmental legislation protect the commons now?*- Mark Dowie

[2] Despite all these measures, the empire suffered several major setbacks in the course of the 6th century. The first one was the plague, which lasted from 541 to 543 AD and, by decimating the empire's population, probably creating a scarcity of labor and a rising of wages, leading to an overall collapse of infrastructure.

being hailed as something new and revolutionary. It is being pounded into our children's heads in schools, and pushed into our homes through media outlets. "The Earth is in trouble" is the mantra of the modern left, and by its sister movement, the Progressives[3]. They tout the benefits of a government planned and controlled society and carry the banners of environmentalism. It is nothing new however, and the current theory of environmentalism and Green politics are little more than dressed up version of ancient feudalism[4] under the royal families, and tyrannical kings of old. It bears little resemblance to the ancient concepts of keeping drinking water and tilling soils clean.

Following the fall of the Roman Empire, in pre-industrial civilizations' national economy, if one could call it that, was based primarily on an economic model known as "feudalism." Although historians debate at great length about the timing and nature of feudalism,

---

[3] Progressivism is a political attitude favoring or advocating changes or reform through governmental action.

[4] Although derived from the Latin word *feodum* (fief), the term *Feudalism* and the system it describes were not conceived of as a formal political system by the people living in the Medieval Period. This is its classic definition, by François-Louis Ganshof (1944).

almost all agree that feudalism has some basic tenets and theories used to govern the economy.

First and foremost, feudalism revolves around a centrally planned society, chiefly from a monarch or monarchical form of government. Resources are owned by the king or the state and redistributed by the monarchical power to the people, or peasants, in the most efficient means for the monarch to maintain wealth and power. How that was accomplished varied from kingdom to kingdom, but the essential concept of monarchical control of resources and its subsequent redistribution, was the primary economic model from shortly after the fall of the Roman Empire until the industrial age. The nature of this economic model also maintained monarchical power for essentially the same period of time.[5] The monarchical power of Europe was chiefly held in the hands of a very few families (heretofore referred to as the Royals), based in the large European kingdoms of France, England, Sweden, Norway and Germany. Although the Russian

---

[5] Marc Bloch (1939), also included not only warrior nobility but peasantry bonds as well and referred to it as a "feudal society". Since 1974 with the publication of Elizabeth A. R. Brown's *The Tyranny of a Construct* and Susan Reynolds' *Fiefs and Vassals* (1994), there has been extensive discussion about the definition of Feudalism.

Royal families were directly related to the European Royal families (they are in fact all related to one another by either birth or marriage), their reclusive nature and distance geographically limited their direct contact on a regular basis.

The use of feudalism as an economic model differed from that of the Roman Empire which relied more on trade and slave labor than it did on direct control of the environment. In Rome individual landowners were plentiful (called *perigrini*[6]) and provided goods or resources to those who could pay the best price for them. There were more similarities in the Roman Empire to modern capitalism than there were to feudalism.

The emergence of feudalism after the Roman collapse was an act mostly out of necessity and circumstance rather than an intellectual theory. As civilization collapsed, local land barons set up shop seizing the land and protecting those around them in exchange for work and wages. Rampant violence and illness ran roughshod over Europe and the local barony

---

[6] *Peregrini* could acquire citizenship and land individually, either through service in the *auxilia* for the minimum 25-year term, or by special grant of the emperor for merit or status. The key person in the grant of citizenship to individuals was the provincial governor.

which eventually developed into the Royals. The nobility was truly the only safe harbor in an essentially lawless society. Environmentalism was a matter of control, not economic theory during this period.

Today economic theory is a question that has taken a left turn, from how best to efficiently manufacture goods with a minimum impact on the environment, to the argument that industry and its expansion is inherently evil and therefore must be minimized. The movement to control and eradicate emissions and pollutants almost completely (commonly known as the Green Movement) has been established in various forms in many industrialized societies. In short, our political and societal growth has stagnated due to the rise of Green power motivations over more traditional economic and environmental concerns.

From an historical point of view the bulk of capitalistic growth and capitalism began in the latter half of the 18th century. Capitalism and its gains are chiefly a contract of American economic expansion, and its greatest gains came under the principle allowance of a free society with minimal controls on its citizenry. This is key to understanding the process of capitalism.

Capitalism achieves its greatest growth and most substantial gains only in a completely free society unfettered by excessive taxation or oversight.

The earliest forms of capitalism were present even in the earliest powerful societies of Caesar's Rome and Ptolemaic Egypt. These cultures, like the economies of post-Renaissance England and Europe, and eventually the United States, relied heavily on the exchange and sale of goods and the conversion of raw material into manufactured goods. But all of these societies, and the earliest part of American growth, relied on enslaved labor to produce its profits. As such it cannot be called a true capitalistic economy but rather an economy built upon slave labor and thus simply another form of conquest economics. Slave labor is not capitalism, at least not in the modern sense.

The fact remains *that only until America rejected slavery as a form of economic production, did the true growth and the full potential of capitalism reveal itself.* The growth of the American economy in its post-Civil War period to today far exceeded the growth of the

---

American economy in the previous 200 years.[7] It is freedom and the concept of limited government and regulation that allowed America to prosper, not a managed society of enslaved workers. With slave labor you have just another form of a managed economy. Slavery can take on many aspects, either by the methods of traditional slavery of the chain and whip or that of feudalistic law and legal bonding to the land. Despite the popular misconception that America was built primarily by slave labor, the vast majority of economic growth which occurred in post-Civil War America was by an efficient use of "cheap" labor (such as immigrant and non-union labor). It was low wages definitely, but wages nevertheless, and the men who worked them did so by choice or circumstance.[8]

The roots of industry, and thus profits, lie in a period of years shortly after the European Reformation of the 1500's and the explosive growth of mechanization

---

[7] Bowman, John. "An Economic Analysis of Midwestern Farm Values and Farm Land Income, 1860-1900." YALE ECONOMIC ESSAYS 5 (1965): 317-52.

[8] The Relative Efficiency of Slave Agriculture: A Comment, Donald F. Schaefer and Mark D. Schmitz, *The American Economic Review* Vol. 69, No. 1 (Mar., 1979), pp. 208-212.

and industrialization that came with it. Although Europe was growing and expanding by leaps and bounds, it was chiefly driven by the flood of new and cheap resources from the New World. As colonization of the New World drained large portions of the European populations, shipload after shipload of resources such as sugar, cotton, furs and gold began to flow into the harbors of Europe. The untold wealth of millions of hectares of undeveloped land was being transferred into the eager hands of European exploration companies and their proprietors. The New World also brought a new concept of governance to the peoples of the world--freemen who formed a new way of financing their lives with capitalism. Although there were substantial aspects of the American economy that were dominated by slave labor, the majority of manufactured goods and raw supply was being contributed by free men who exploited the vast tracts of open land for profit.

Gone were the days that men were tethered to the lands through grants of lands from the monarchy. A settler could exchange only a few years of his life in exchange for the ability to own outright their own land and reap the profits themselves. Although those first few years were enduring hardship, the rewards of being essentially free from the onerous laws and taxes of the crown made the risks bearable. Once the debt was paid off a freeman could ply a trade or move into other lands. There were no limits to the amount of land a man could claim for himself provided he could work it and defend it. In fact, the Royals of Europe encouraged expansion in the New World--provided it was done in the name of the king. The monarchs believed that the substantial acquisition of new lands without the prospect of expensive wars could relieve the ever growing burden of expensive armies with a virtually endless flow of raw supplies and cheap manufactured goods.

Unfortunately for the Royals, because of the distances and the difficulties of travel and communication, it became virtually impossible to govern the New World colonies as directly as they governed their homelands. As a result, most of the new territories and colonies were left to govern themselves, albeit with territorial governorships that reported directly back to the crown. And because of the distances involved, it was impractical to give direct representation in Parliamentary government to the new colonies. Colonial governors and viceroys were given almost dictatorial powers, and as long as the flow of goods kept coming back to the homeland, little was said about the methods used to govern.

It was the application of the law in a strong government versus an independent people, rather than the free hand of conservatism and capitalism, that was the single most contributing factor that led not only to the American Revolution of 1776. Had England not expanded the role of government in colonial America, it is unlikely the Revolution would have occurred in the manner it, or at the time that it did. The very type of independent minded people that had made the New World lands so profitable and enriching to the crown were now the downfall of the monarchy. By expanding the Royal coffers through colonization, and then substantially increasing taxes and regulation, they had essentially now created their own built in rebellion. Governors and colonial viceroys became increasingly pressured to provide higher and higher levels of supplies back to the mother countries of Spain, England and France. The crowns were beginning to demand gold directly from the colonists in the form of taxation of the supplies and goods they provided. The profits the Royals were gaining from the goods coming in from the colonies were simply not enough to pay the bills of large standing armies and navies. The Royals were warring with each other in Europe and massive amounts of gold were needed to build new gunpowder based weaponry and to pay troops to prevent desertions.

This is probably the most crucial period of world economic development because individuals now became less reliant upon the Royals for support and protection, and the power of the Royals over society began to wane. Thus as New World colonists travelled to lands farther and farther away, and more profitable enterprises became available, they were no longer dependent upon the Royals for their livelihood or protection. This soon became quite apparent to the Royals that were fast growing less relevant in American society. This element of "government protection" against the hazards of the world would pop up again later in the Progressive Movement some 100 years later.

Up until 1776 monarchical rule had sway over Europe for more than 1,000 years. The link to a planned society as the principal form of economic growth and government was not only essential to the power brokers of the Royals, it was the foundation for society. Furthermore, the use of feudalism and societal planning had been used for so long was taken for granted as the *only* form of legitimate government. This presumption of power and its subsequent assumption of legitimacy is eventually what weakened the Royals by the late 17th century and contributed greatly to the rise of industrialization and mechanization. The Royals central thesis to power revolved around a concept known as the "divine right of kings [9]" in which the authority they were granted came directly from God. With that divine right came the responsibility of providing for the common good. This protection and provision for the common good was the chief source of power for the Royals, based on central economic model of feudalism. Feudalism's economic tenets, however, revolve around the central

---

[9] The **divine right of kings** is a political and religious doctrine of royal and political legitimacy. It asserts that a monarch is subject to no earthly authority, deriving his right to rule directly from the will of God. The king is thus not subject to the will of his people, the aristocracy, or any other estate of the realm, including (in the view of some, especially in Protestant countries) the Church. According to this doctrine, since only God can judge an unjust king, the king can do no wrong. The doctrine implies that any attempt to depose the king or to restrict his powers runs contrary to the will of God and may constitute a sacrilegious act.

thesis that a king is the supreme monarch and he derives his authority from God. The king, therefore, owns and maintains the land surrounding his central area of sway; typically a fortification such as a castle or keep. All that the king controls he controls through force of action such as an army or troops, and his control exists primarily to protect the lands from destruction. Along with it comes the understanding that the minions, or peasants that live and work the land are under his control as well. The king then redistributes the wealth of the land for the betterment of society as a whole.

The feudalistic economic model is in this respect similar to modern day Socialism or Communism. The good of the whole is of far more worth than the value of the individual. The support and long term existence of these societies, in fact, depends on it. The king is its chief architect passing down his authority from generation to generation through family heirs. Great pains were made to ensure the line would continue, and great sums were spent to educate and train men (and women) for the task of running the kingdom which included other branches of

---

government such as the nobility[10]. A noble would never protect the rights of a peasant over the kingdom's rule of law. In feudalistic times life was cheap and often very brief due to the lack of medical care (at least in modern terms) and the nature of a lifetime of physical labor devoted solely to the enrichment of the king and his nobles.

The prospect of an enemy, a group of barbarians or even illness or disease wiping out a village was very real in medieval Europe. A baron or king could provide protection against those dangers either through direct military protection or an educated understanding of medical and safety protocols. Thus the peasants were not only dependent upon the king for wages but for all aspects of their lives, and they needed the king as much as the king needed the peasant labor. Protection is a key element to an understanding of modern day political Progressivism as well. Only government can protect you from the evils of low quality food, environmental

---

[10] Nobility is a state-privileged status which is generally hereditary. The privileges associated with nobility may constitute substantial advantages over non-nobles, and may be largely honorary, but are maintained, or at least officially acknowledged, by law or government of a monarchy.

dangers, law enforcement, etc. Liberal leaders love to issue laws, bureaus and regulations to "protect" society from the evils of the world, and thus maintain their own hegemony over the peasantry. Liberals believe that government leaders (from Congress, Parliament or other forms of modern government) were smarter and better equipped to handle these hazards than the peasantry and thus the task must fall onto them. This is the intellectual basis for liberal politics, and justification for the existence for these social structures. Progressivism in this regard is identical to feudalism, and this is why today's Royals support liberal theories and liberal leadership--the king knows best.

Key to this task was to ensure the heir-apparent was educated with the best tutors and trained properly in the martial arts of combat and war. In fact, during the high point of feudalistic sway, it was only the king, or the nobles that could read or write. Exceptions, of course, were the churches and priests who were educated in order to pass their legacy of religious education from generation to generation. Since the Church was the only other educated class in medieval times they soon became a legitimate power, and historically they became an obstacle to monarchical supremacy up until modern times. Kings kept fealty and interest in the Church only insofar as it kept the populous happy and in tune with their faith. Kings rarely had actually faith in God or Church--it was simply a matter of populist politics.

The Royals defined themselves through this education, much as the Church did, and enormous sums were spent by both factions to maintain that education by funding tradesman and craftsman unions. Artisans who excelled in the crafting of goods or masons were not nobles, but their education and training led most of them to earn freeman status which was highly valued by kings. There are substantial historical records to indicate educated men were as prized to the king as the gold they plundered from the lands they invaded. Technology, much like today, was critical to success, and reliance on technology rather than God was emblematic of nobility whereas the masses viewed technology as magic and were subject to superstition. Support of the traditional crafting and tradesman unions were critical to the success of the Royals. The concept of royal support for trade unions is still seen today again in liberal politics. Without the power of organized labor and the technological innovations of trade labor, the Royals would lose an important advantage in wars and a substantial amount of their power base.

It is this theory in which leadership is better educated and trained and therefore better suited to run the kingdom that we also see today in modern liberal thought. The common viewpoint today held by the left, particularly the American left, is that the only proper political view for an educated person is Liberalism. Modern colleges and other schools of higher education are the training grounds for Liberalism, and while there are many colleges that do not blend their politics with their education, by and large American colleges foster and promote Liberalism.

Liberals believe that Conservatism has its roots in religious and rural thought, that it is limited in its depth and a product of a low upbringing or education. This theory goes back to the traditional confrontational relationship between the Royals and the Church[11]. Most modern institutions of higher learning also give credence to this concept as its educators cling to the notion that superior education equals superior wisdom. They firmly believe that a society is better run by those who have the intelligence and background to do so. All men are not created equal under the mantra of liberals. There are some that are superior or of *noble* birth, and it is these people that must run our society, not the common man. It is the belief of the Royals that allowing the masses to govern themselves leads to chaos and ruin.

This is a central theme in Progressivism; that Conservatism (or its sister Libertarianism) revolves not around education or collegiate schooling but in rural and uneducated training. The issue that Liberalism is anti-Church and views people finding solace in their Bibles as somehow substandard is no coincidence and has its roots chiefly from the conflicts between the Royals and the

---

[11] The structure and theology of the church was a matter of fierce dispute for generations. These disputes were finally ended by a coup d'état (the "Glorious Revolution") in 1688 from which emerged a church polity with an established church and a number of non-conformist churches whose members at first suffered various civil disabilities which were only removed over time, as did the substantial minority who remained Roman Catholic in England whose church organization remained illegal until the 19th century.

Church in feudalistic times. Although the Church in that period was made up of educated men, perhaps even more so than the Royals, the majority of its worshippers certainly were not. The Church acted as champions of the masses in their power struggles against the Royals. This was only natural since the Church's viewpoint was that freedom came inherently from God and not from kings and that thinking is antithetical to the power of the Royals.

The theory of elitism and nobility of class is manifested not only in Progressivism but also in the Green Movement. The Greens believe that mankind, if left to its own devices, would destroy and ruin the very environment in which we live in order to gain more profits from an enterprise. They also believe, as do the Royals, that resources and growth are best managed from a central authority, that the lands belong not to the individual that settles or owns them, but to society as a whole or a central authority such as government, or the modern day equivalent of "state." Statism, whereby the individual is subservient to the state, is the central and preeminent goal of Progressivism. Society is managed from a centralized planning source, and it fits neatly into the age-old society model of feudalism which plans society around a central authority figure. A planned society is how the Royals managed their own lands up until the late 1700's and it was how they maintained power for so long and with such strength. Thus Progressivism, green politics and the Royals all have as their central thesis a planned society under a single government--the very definition of tyranny.

The concept of basic environmentalism should not be confused with the political movement of the Greens. Before Progressivism and its sister theory Statism began to take hold in American society, industrialists were well aware of the problems of pollution and environmental damage. However, they saw pollution as something else. They saw it as waste, and the reduction of pollutants would not only be popular among consumers, but would lead to more profits as less resources went to waste. A clean burning power plant was also an efficient one and the move to more efficient manufacturing methods had already begun by the mid-19th and early 20th centuries. Long before Greens made the move toward the limiting of economic growth, industry was making cleaner factories. The factory of the 1940's bore little resemblance to the factory of the 1840's. Workers were given cleaner and safer areas to work and factories recycled waste into more useful byproducts. While unions were primarily concerned with the actual working conditions of its individual members, it was the corporations themselves that sought to increase profits through faster working and cleaner running equipment. By the time Ralph Nader came along, factory foremen and engineers had for years already been looking to shave a few more cents on the dollar by producing a better product and had made substantial strides toward cleaner and more efficient factories. The issue of environmental and safety protections for the workers was an issue of profits to them, not politics. The introduction of environmental and safety regulations set by an arbitrary third party did little except to increase the costs of productivity.

Economist Milton Freidman has postulated correctly that politics in manufacturing has actually led to dirtier and less safe products, albeit it has made changes on a faster and more radical scale. Milton Friedman on Ralph Nader:

*The great danger to the consumer is the monopoly -- whether private or governmental. His most effective protection is free competition at home and free trade throughout the world. The consumer is protected from being exploited by one seller by the existence of another seller from whom he can buy and who is eager to sell to him. Alternative sources of supply protect the consumer far more effectively than all the Ralph Naders of the world* (Milton Friedman, *Phil Donohue Show*, 1979).

The hard truth of environmentalism is that today we would have safer, cheaper and less polluting cars had government NOT gotten involved in the manufacture of products about which it knows nothing. CAFÉ regulations on automobiles have made them heavier, less efficient and more expensive than what free market economics dictate and slowed the advance of cleaner, more economical cars. The modern internal combustion motor has fuel efficiency and environmental controls on it that are, quite frankly, antiques primarily due to the government setting arbitrary rules. In most states emissions testing facilities remain open despite the fact that cars are thousands of times cleaner today than they were just 25 years ago[12].

Modern Progressive thought purports there are some people that are better than others, either by birth, circumstance or education, much as the Royals do. This concept is promoted in order to enable those that have similar Progressive opinions in power. They feel that they have the moral and legal right to be in positions of authority. Many leaders of the Progressive[13] Movement, as well as the Green Movement, believe this to be true. They view modern American rural political thought to be devoid of intellectual value. The Greens or Progressives see the average American voter as an ignorant redneck hillbilly, and thus devalues their libertarian thought as being the thought process of the uneducated masses just as the Royals viewed those who followed the Church. This elitism is a significant part of liberal political theory

---

[12] *Clean Cars in California: Four Decades of Progress in the Unfinished Battle to Clean up Our Air*, Nov 2010.

[13] Progressivism is a political attitude favoring or advocating changes or reform through governmental action. The Progressive Movement began in cities with settlement workers and reformers who were interested in helping those facing harsh conditions at home and at work.

in the same way that monarchs viewed the serfdom of their own period. The kings, queens and other monarchical positions of authority such as barons and dukes, often took the viewpoint that if they did not take care of the peasants, they would be unable to do so for themselves. Many writers of the period from 1650 to 1800, particularly those of England and Germany and to a lesser extent France, wrote that America would not be able to survive without a king to govern the mobs. Of course history proved their arguments to be false, but the sentiment remained--the mobs are unable to decide what is best for themselves.

Over the last century the argument for the restoration of the monarchy has gone largely ignored, but the actions of Progressivism, which have enormous influence on modern European governments, has been the opposite. Most of the European Union (as it now is called in more parochial circles) favors strong handed government intervention in the economic affairs of state. More interestingly, there has been a significant movement in the last 50 years for more governmental control in the areas of environment and pollution. The control of resources, and the distribution of them to men and industries willing to pay fealty or tribute to the government, is no different than the concept of feudalistic control from the previous 1500 years of human development.

And control is the word. Although from a scientific point of view the world we live in may be changing, either in the form of global warming or cooling, the political aspect of industrial control has been substantially more onerous than the evidence would suggest. Consider the massive drain on a nation's resources if you were to slow industrial output by a mere 10%. Imagine how much more tax revenues are lost. The United States GDP in 2009 was a stunning $14.15 trillion. Ten percent of that would be $1.41 trillion--more than enough to pay for free healthcare for everyone, pay off the shockingly high national debt or completely fund the national defense. At $1.41 trillion a year it would also pay for 100% of federal discretionary spending. This means every government bureau, minus Medicare, Social

Security and Defense would be paid for--astonishing when it is defined in those terms[14].

American society today is based on a government that was established to be free of tyrannical monarchical forces that reigned in Europe at the time. The law here in America, particularly at the time of the American Revolution, was applied unequally to the colonists. Taxes were levied upon the colonists who had little say in their application. Taxes were also levied against them unfairly and unequally in comparison to their mainland counterparts. A good argument could be made that had the monarchy allowed American representation in Parliament, the collapse and eventual American Revolution might not have ever happened.

In the establishment of our government the American founding fathers put severe limits on the ability of government to expand its powers over the individual states and the American people in general. The Constitution was a unique document at the time, and still

---

[14] Data sources: World Bank, World Development Indicators - Last updated December 21, 2010. The subsequent **2010 Financial Report of the United States Government**, reporting on the implementation of the 2010 Budget, shows a net operating cost of $2,080 billion.

is, because it is the only establishing governmental document that puts limits on the government rather than on the people. It allows for the individual states and their residents to arm themselves and speak freely which were unheard of concepts at the time. Many countries today have distinct and defined limits on what their citizenry may and may not do, whereas in the United States the Constitution defines what government may or may not do. This is a radical departure from previous government charters.

Strict conservative theory adheres to those principles of limited government and limiting government. Most importantly they stand by strict and equal adherence to the law. To a Conservative a law must be applied equally or it is, by definition, an unjust and unfair law. It is why, more often than not, a Conservative is viewed as the *law and order* political viewpoint. Even though Liberals also believe in crime prevention and application of criminal law equally, many times the left will make exceptions to the rule of law in order to foment a political viewpoint. Environmental applications and adjustments in the economy work in this way, such as the theory of cap and trade[15]. The government determines whether or not a business is clean or dirty by an arbitrary set of rules then punishes those companies accordingly through regulatory rules and fines. However, companies may buy out of those fines and rules by paying fees to buy *credits* in order to offset their fines from being dirty. Those heavy polluters go on destroying the environment with no incentive to run their industry cleaner or more efficiently. Such a system actually rewards poor performance and punishes companies that invest in more efficient technologies.

Remarkably one can point back again to the Royals influence in these types of cap and trade policies as they are astonishingly similar to policies in the Middle Ages in regards to sin and punishment within the Church. In those days a noble or monarch could simply buy credits with the Church to offset their sins of rape, murder and theft. These *indulgences*, as they were called

---

[15] Emissions trading (also known as cap and trade) is a market-based approach used to control pollution by providing economic incentives for achieving reductions in the emissions of pollutants. A central authority (usually a governmental body) sets a limit or cap on the amount of a pollutant that can be emitted. The limit or cap is allocated or sold to firms in the form of emissions permits which represent the right to emit or discharge a specific volume of the specified pollutant.

then, simply offset the punishments of imprisonment, excommunication and eternal damnation through the payment of monies to the state and church. This too subsidized and institutionalized the issue of sin and crime in feudal Europe. The similarities of cap and trade and feudal indulgences are no coincidence. They work identically and have the same end result--an enrichment of the state at the cost of equality under the law.

As another modern day example there is the issue of illegal immigration. Conservative political theory is in support of the strict application of the law. You must be born here or apply through the citizenship process to be a legal citizen of the United States. This is an equal application of the law. Everyone has the same ability, and chance to be an American citizen. Those that work hard to come here are welcome and in fact encouraged.

Liberal sensibilities lean toward a "feel good" solution rather than what the law proscribes. They feel that since conditions are bad in Mexico and illegal immigrants are merely seeking a better life for themselves and their families, they have a right to break the law and emigrate here to work and live. The law is an obstacle to a Liberal; an obstacle to achieving justice in an unjust society--whereas to a Conservative, the law itself is the definition of justice. The Conservative believes that if the Liberal feels the system is unjust they can change it through the ballot box or through legislation; whereas the Liberal will simply encourage the breaking of the law. The rights of "morality" supersede the equal application of law. And as earlier argument shows, such a belief merely enriches one group of individuals at the expense of others. Consider the point that many companies and businesses benefit from the massive influx of cheap labor while others who legitimately run businesses cannot compete and are forced into bankruptcy. Again, this unequal application of law under the guise of morality and good government not only disrupts the economy but encourages and institutionalizes normal economic growth.

This is the same attitude on a myriad of issues. Health care is a right thus we must pass new rules enabling millions of Americans access to health insurance (but interestingly and hypocritically enough, not health care itself). The convicted murderer must not be executed because it is unjust due to the killer's childhood history of abuse and neglect. Our taxes must be more heavily applied to wealthier people because its unfair for some people to have more money than others-- ignoring the fact that those people either worked harder or worked smarter to achieve their success. Racial tensions are stirred up in order to defend the position that racial discrimination is acceptable as long as it benefits the minority in the form of affirmative action laws.

The argument is endless and deliberately circular. The law is something to get around, twist through legal maneuver or just plain ignore in order to mollify their own sense of monarchical and elitist self worth. This is why self-esteem is pushed in our Liberal controlled schools rather than facts, figures and basic studies. A person who has had their self-esteem pumped through controlling education is more likely to be manipulated into a false sense of moral inequality, rather than teaching the basic concepts of free thought. (It is interesting that Nazi's used it to instill superiority in their children.) Laws that strangle freedom of speech are promoted in order to break the independent spirit of self-reliance and responsibility. The limits of the Constitution are rules to be rewritten not obeyed. This is the mantra of the left and Progressives.

The age of the crusading activist is drowning out the voice of the Minutemen.

This is central to the difference between a Liberal and a Conservative. This is why it is the Liberal who defends the rights of a murderer but wants stronger punishments for traffic violations. It is why they want labor unions to break private enterprise and deny corporations equal rights to public issues while promoting laws that allow unions to play politics. It is about leveling the playing field, not through equal application of the law, but rather by dealing the playing cards from the bottom of the deck. Manipulation of the masses and the economy is nothing new to the monarchs of Europe; it is a game for them as old as time, and it is how they have maintained their power for centuries.

But in order to understand the relationship between monarchical control and environmentalism, one has to view the issue from the point of view of 15th century finances as well as modern day application of the law under Liberalism. In the days of Feudalism the Royals had complete ownership of the lands surrounding their castle and under their military control. The forests belonged to the king as did the streams and resources that

---

came from it. The nobility were merely stewards of the land in respect to the king, and his power came directly from God in the form of birthright. It was by this legal justification that the king could raise taxes drawn from the peasants in either the form of wages or bodies in the time of war. Despite the absolute power of the king each of his powers had a legal and moral justification to them. Thus control of resources was the true power behind the crown. If a king could not raise gold in the form of taxes on the resources harvested, he could not pay the troops to maintain his power, and anarchy would ensue. Insofar as that is concerned, the cry for a return to feudalism by monarchs and their descendents is true--there would be chaos and anarchy without government. But the role of government in the view of American political thought is one of guidance and protection not control, at least not until recently.

According to the Oxford History of Britain[16] (1999), anarchy is exactly what happened with the loss of power by the nobility in England. The nobility began to sell off lands for enormous short-term profits as the age

---

[16] Oxford History of Britain, Chapters 5-6, 8.

of industrialization swept across Europe. A noble might make a fair amount taxing the lands but stood to make a tidy windfall for the crown if the lands were turned over to budding industrialists who could mine and farm the land much more efficiently than the king. The lure of easy and large amounts of gold was hard to resist to kings who lived a lavish and expensive lifestyle of debauchery and hedonism and needed to support expensive wars being fought over those now obscenely valuable lands. In the end, although the royal coffers were temporarily swelling with gold, it made it almost impossible for the crown to raise taxes and gold in succeeding generations. Massive debt ensued when future kings were unable to directly tap the lands for gold to pay for wars; wars that were essential to protecting lands and providing food and shelter to peasants.

Green politics is being used as a tool now; a tool to control and effectively hamstring the growth of industrial societies which leads to a bigger question. Who or what is behind the massive push to limit the growth of industry and reduce industry or even altogether eliminate it? The reasons for this are various, but there is substantial evidence to indicate that the movement toward a more environmentally friendly society, and the Environmental Movement as a whole, has been pirated by those who would seek to use the argument of environmental protection to increase their own wealth and power. This is the difference between the traditional environmental school of thought and the Greens of today. It is no longer about the true protection of the environment, as it is about the destruction of capitalism.

To understand this you have to look at not only who would benefit from this change but also at its root causes and foundations. The careful student of history has to seriously consider the greater forces at work that would effectively gain by a reduction of profitability or grow in power as the power of industry captains and profits waned. In short, the reader must ask themselves this central question: Who would benefit most by the destruction of industrial and capitalistic growth, and who was hurt the most by the explosive growth of Capitalism and industrialism from the late 17th century until today? How would a return to a more feudalistic economy be beneficial to the powers that are promoting it?

The move to toward modern, Green economic policies and the subsequent regulation and control of private industry is heavily supported and funded by the Royals and also by the wealthy landed gentry of Europe. Prince Charles himself writes often on the issue of green economic policy and recently published a treatise on modern green economic theories called *"Harmony"* (2010). In *"Harmony,"* Charles takes the traditional position of royal control of the forests and lands in the sense that peasants cannot be trusted to run the lands properly and like the locust will deplete the resources for their own economic gain rather than look at the long-term implications of over fishing and over farming. Prince Charles goes on to use the term revolution when discussing the position of environmentalism and how it would fundamentally revert 500 years of economic success and theory and firmly put the control of resources back into the hands of government:

> *Revolution is a strong word and I use it deliberately. The many environmental and social problems that now loom large on our horizon cannot be solved by carrying on with the very approach that caused them....This will involve our taking all sorts of dramatic steps to change*

*the way we consider the world and how we act in it...* (Prince Charles, Harmony, 2010).

The resounding cry of the Royals is clear in this passage. We must indeed revert back to a monarchical form of government and turn our resources back over to the hands of those who know how to handle it best (i.e. the king or as times have changed now, the government). From the wonks that now are the noble families of Europe the message is clear--liberty and freedom must be destroyed, and the power of the individual must succumb to the boot of sanitarian control.

If a peasant shot a king's deer or fished from a royal stream without legal permissions from the nobility, the penalties were often harsh and sometimes lethal. Control of the resources were managed from the viewpoint that without those royal controls the peasants would simply chop down every forest and fish out every stream and hunt the deer until extinct and thus reduce the kings ability to raise funds. What this viewpoint and this line of political thought fails to realize is the farming of resources is done at a profit, and the profit motive precludes the majority of this behavior. An industrialist that owns a forest and farms the timber for logs to sell at market consistently replaces those forests with new ones through replanting and does not use clear cutting techniques. Thus the timber tycoon maintains his wealth by using the forest as a renewable resource rather than pillaging the land as the Progressives would like people to think.

Power is a thing that is difficult to earn and twice as hard to give up. The Royals of Europe had held sway over the peoples of Britain, Germany, Scandinavia, France and Eastern Europe for almost 1500 years before a small group of independent minded patriots in a backwater colony of the British Empire decided to throw off the yoke of monarchical oppression and declare themselves free men under the eyes of God. In a short 70-year period following the American Revolution most of the Royal families of Europe had either lost their power or lost their heads to a wave of popular excitement over the notion that all men were created equally and the newfound wealth of living a life of freedom and capitalism.

The royal houses of most nations were almost entirely wiped out in the cataclysmic years following the

American Revolution. This left England and the Scandinavian nations of Norway and Sweden to carry the banner of monarchy and feudalism into the 19th century. Even the reclusive Romanov dynasty of Russia soon fell to the tides of a populist movement under the oppressive yoke of Communism. These two holdouts of traditional Royal power were forced to make significant compromises both to their wealth and power in order to survive the avalanche of Capitalism that swept through Europe. Though the blue blood thrones of these nations remained relatively intact, entire orders of baronies, duchies and the Royal progression were virtually annihilated.

The lone holdouts of England and Scandinavia, and to a lesser extent France and Spain, developed a deep grudge against what they perceived as antithetical to proper societal development, and the natural order of monarchical rule. They viewed monarchical rule as the divine order of things, not independent capitalism, despite American claims that the rights of free men came from God and not government.

This is what made American independence unique. Rebellions against the crown had risen before and failed in almost every sovereign nation of Europe. In every one of those rebellions, either the rebels failed to instill a sense of purpose in their rebellion against the concept of monarchy, or their fledgling government fell into disrepair and new kings were restored from the bloodlines of the old. In each case they still held to the notion that it was the king that was with divine inspiration, not men.

America was unique in this respect from then until now and has been the only government that has been established by law and document that limits the power of government--where the natural order of mankind is not one of monarchical rule but independence and freedom. This is key to understanding the power of the American Revolution. Under other forms of representative government there was still the understanding that the king was divine, even in post-Magna Carta England. This link to the divine spirit and authority of the king was considered necessary by previous rebellion governments as a method of establishing the legitimacy of their rebellion. Without the understanding and tacit approval of God to maintain a royal line, men feared their rebellions' new government would not be recognized by the people.

The American Constitution is the chief culprit in the minds of the current royal houses and its framers are the villains of their undoing. It mattered not that the exceptional wealth of industrialization and capitalism were the financiers of the American Revolution--this could be managed even under monarchical rule. The key to the restoration of royal power and the return of a centrally feudal power to the hands of royalty would have to come at the destruction of the American Constitution and the American way of life--there could be no halfway measure. A free and ungovernable people would be impossible to manage in a feudal system and only through the degradation and destruction of free thought and rights established by God, not by men, could the Royals hope to regain power.

Capitalism could be a valuable tool in a managed monarchy and was proven as a successful model for the future in 20th century Europe. Although the peoples of Europe accepted such change to their society in an almost silent revolution and conversion from free democracies into socialist and managed republics, America would be more problematic. Its people were decedents of the framers of the Constitution and the pioneers and religious zealots of the 17th century, and they were protected by a document that was granite solid in its protections and its immutability. The control and effective castration of American and capitalistic thought and processes is not the primary motivating factor of the individual environmentalist today except in the extreme cases of radicals or militants.

This political theory was hatched long ago but now was corrupted by a source that was not entirely anticipated or expected by America. It is the economic backing by the Royals of Europe of the Green Movement that is now seeking to disarm and destroy capitalism for their own purposes. More importantly this is not their first try at it--the last time it was attempted it resulted in two World Wars and tens of millions of lost lives as the forces that be would involve themselves in a titanic struggle over that control versus the free activities of individuals.

The questions are: What is the link between the modern Greens, and the traditional Royal houses of Europe? How is it that the noble political ideology of protecting the environment from self-destructive overdevelopment could be perverted into a tool that is being used to destroy capitalism--and why?

To understand this we must first look at what happened to the Royal houses as the American Revolution changed the political landscape and capitalism took hold as the primary form of economic growth. The problem was a rich one but then nothing would be insurmountable given enough time and money.

Unfortunately for America, the remaining Royals of Europe had plenty of both.

# The Germans

*Our German Fatherland to which I hope will be granted . . . to become in the future as closely united, as powerful, and as authoritative as once the Roman world-empire was, and that, just as in the old times they said, "Civis romanus sum," hereafter, at some time in the future, they will say, "I am a German citizen."- Kaiser Wilhelm II*

It is no secret that the German royal family is the progenitor and defining link of most of the current royal families in Europe and also is directly related to the current monarch of England, Elizabeth II. If the Royals of Europe were a tree and Elizabeth a branch, then the ancestral Prussian[17] royal houses could certainly be called the trunk of that tree.

The key to understanding many of what motivates the Royals is what gives sustenance to those branches and feeds the trunk of that great tree. The great tree of the Royals has at its center the German royal houses. To

---

[17] **Prussia** was a German kingdom and historic state originating out of the Duchy of Prussia and the Margraviate of Brandenburg. For centuries, this state had important influence on German and European history. The last capital of the Prussian state was Berlin.

understand this tree of the Royals and the resultant collapse from two World Wars which also led to the rise of Communism, we need to turn back the clock a bit to just past the American Revolution and look at the turmoil in Europe caused by the fall of the French crown of the Bourbons and the rise of Napoleon.

As said earlier the American Revolution was acting as a catalyst for the fall of the French king (the Bourbons) and the rise of the bloodthirsty Napoleon who was seeking to destroy all the original lineages of the French Royals and place himself as the new de facto King of France, or titular Emperor[18]. After declaring himself emperor, Napoleon moved against his neighbor Russia in an attempt to consolidate his victories in Europe and marched across the German, Austrian and Prussian borders ignoring their conquest and moving deeper inland.

---

[18] On the advice of Talleyrand, Napoleon ordered the kidnapping of Louis Antoine, Duke of Enghien, in violation of neighboring Baden's sovereignty. After a secret trial the Duke was executed, even though he had not been involved in the plot. Napoleon used the plot to justify the re-creation of a hereditary monarchy in France, with himself as emperor, as a Bourbon restoration would be more difficult if the Bonapartist succession was entrenched in the constitution.

Had Napoleon succeeded in conquering Russia, he most certainly would have turned his attention to the Prussian states of Austria, Hungary and Romania. These states, although suffering from the Napoleonic wars, did not come under the direct thumb of Napoleon, and so the royal lines were essentially preserved. The Franco-Prussian treaty of 1812 established some protections for the Prussian (German) lineage and supplied troops to the beleaguered Napoleon in his wars in Europe. But Napoleon's failure in Russia, now put the onus on the Germans to move forward against the French little corporal and thus broke the treaty to pursue him across Germany.

The Royal House of Prussia, the Hohenzollerns, knew full well that a massive defeat by Napoleon was imminent if they did not act quickly, and German sovereignty in the region might be damaged beyond repair. It was decided that the German houses should mobilize against the fleeing Napoleon[19].

King Frederick Wilhelm acted with decisive bold action and moved against Napoleon with Prussian troops under the leadership of Blücher and Gneisenau which proved vital at the Battles of Leipzig (1813) and Waterloo (1815). German supremacy was once again established in the region, and with France in chaos from the collapse of Napoleon, Wilhelm and the Germans were now poised to become the supreme rulers of the European region economically, geographically and politically. King Frederick Wilhelm had successfully unified Germany under a single monarch.

Yet Wilhelm the First did not press the advantage left to him by the retreat of Napoleon and chose instead to allow the further weakening of the traditional monarchy, and feudalistic control of the economy was allowed to collapse under the now firmly entrenched

---

[19] Following Napoleon's failed invasion of Russia and his defeats in the Peninsular War, the anti-French forces had cautiously regrouped as the Sixth Coalition comprised of Russia, Austria, Prussia, Sweden, Britain, Spain, Portugal and certain smaller German states. In total the Coalition could put into the field well over a million troops—indeed by the time of Leipzig, the total Allied armies east of the Rhine probably exceeded a million. By contrast Napoleon's forces had shrunk to just a few hundred thousand.

civilian governments of Europe. Europe breathed a sigh of relief as finally peace might be able to gain momentum in the wake of the bloody French revolution and Napoleon. Wilhelm I passed various anti-Socialism laws and installed Otto Von Bismarck as prime minister to see to the affairs of the fledgling German empire.

There was only a brief respite from Napoleon before the rumblings of power and the monarchy rose to the top again in Central Europe. In 1888 the death of Wilhelm I left a power vacuum for the first time in central Europe since Napoleon. His son, Wilhelm II , the first grandchild of Victoria of the United Kingdom and sixth in the British line of succession at the time of his birth, had planned for a Royal expansion and return to a monarchical form of government, both in Germany and worldwide. This was against the wishes of prime minister Otto von Bismarck, who saw such returns to Royal sway and the expansion of socialism in Germany as dangerous, and could lead to widespread instability, to say nothing of outright war.

The Kaiser, as he came to be known, did not hold to his father's concept of a civilian government running the day to day affairs of the German empire and felt that a

---

true return to monarchical power meant he had to take a more active role in governing. Much to Bismarck's dismay, and against the prime minister's advice, he wanted to restore monarchical power across Europe through aggressive expansion and imperialism.

The rise of Kaiser Wilhelm II was central to the current political theater of today and formed the primary thesis for a return to monarchical form of government and return to feudalism. His political moves would serve as a blueprint for success, both then and today, as the method by which monarchs could hope to regain the power they had held for over a thousand years in Europe. This is probably the central most argument that can be made: had Napoleon not failed in his bid for power and had the Kaiser not risen to power through the use of new social systems and funding of a leftist agenda, Europe might have avoided two World Wars, and Communism would not be the widespread form of government in East.

The effect of the Kaiser's actions cannot be understated and is a point of great controversy from an historical point of view. The Kaiser could not have anticipated the affect he would have or that he would succeed in his goals beyond his wildest imagination--

albeit his success was actually his own personal undoing and cost tens of millions of lives worldwide.

Upon ascension to the throne, the Kaiser made a few direct changes to German society that ring loudly in connection with today's socially left movement and the current German Green Party. The Kaiser hypothesized that a successful monarch could return to power if it had the support of the people under the guise of social restructuring and social justice. The power of the mob is an essentially irresistible force in power politics, and the Kaiser decided to exploit this using the power of the purse. The Socialization Movement of the Kaiser in post-Napoleonic Europe was as revolutionary an idea as America's own move toward Capitalism and democracy.

Kaiser Wilhelm's first actions were enumerating the office of Chancellor who was responsible to the king and replacing him with a British-style cabinet with ministers responsible to the Reichstag. Government policy would be based on the consensus of the cabinet, rather than under the direction of a prime minister. Wilhelm's father once described the new Imperial Constitution as "ingeniously contrived chaos." This chaos would serve the Kaiser well in the coming years, and was intentional to establish his throne as the only bastion of stability, in an ever decreasingly stable society.

The Kaiser shared the outlook of the new Progressive Party[20], and Bismarck was haunted by the fear that should the old Emperor (Wilhelm I) die they would call on one of the Progressive leaders to become Chancellor. [21]

When the Kaiser was in his early twenties, Bismarck tried to separate him from his more militaristic upbringing with some success[22]. Bismarck planned to use the young prince as a weapon against his parents in order to retain his own political dominance. Wilhelm II thus

---

[20] The Progressive Party of 1912 was an American political party. It was formed after a split in the Republican Party between President William Howard Taft and former President Theodore Roosevelt. The main work of the convention was the platform, which set forth the new party's appeal to the voters. It included a broad range of social and political reforms advocated by progressives. In the social sphere the platform called for a national health service to include all existing government medical agencies, social insurance, to provide for the elderly, the unemployed, and the disabled, limited injunctions in strikes, and workers' compensation for work-related injuries.

[21] Michael Balfour, The Kaiser and his Times, Houghton Mifflin (1964) p. 70.

[22] As a scion of the Royal house of Hohenzollern, Wilhelm was also exposed from an early age to the military society of the Prussian aristocracy. This had a major impact on him and, in maturity, Wilhelm was seldom to be seen out of uniform. The hyper-masculine military culture of Prussia in this period did much to frame Wilhelm's political ideals as well as his personal relationships.

---

developed a dysfunctional relationship with his parents, but especially with his English mother. In an outburst in April 1889, which the Empress Victoria conveyed in a letter to her mother Queen Victoria, Wilhelm angrily implied that "an English doctor killed my father, and an English doctor crippled my arm--which is the fault of my mother" who allowed no German physicians to attend to herself or her immediate family[23]. The suggestion that the Kaiser was himself mentally unstable is a matter of some conjecture. Considering the changes that he fomented in German society and his aggressive expansionist policies, there is good argument for it. However, when one considers his ability to consolidate power in his throne and his disruption of his political enemies, the amount of failures that could be contributed to mental illness are minimal--in the same way one could call Napoleon mentally ill. Unstable, perhaps, but he was hardly deficient.

One of the key factors in the formation of the young Kaiser's political motivations can be seen in his response to the mine strike of 1890. Acting against the

[23] Buchner, Max. Wilhelm II, Seine Weltanschauung [Wilhelm II, his world-view]. Leipzig: Verlag von K.F. Koehler.

wishes of the now aging Chancellor Bismarck, the Kaiser intervened on behalf of the miners who felt their living conditions and working conditions were substandard, and he supported them in their bid against the mining companies. He was dubbed the "Labor Emperor" and many of the social systems he established for the miners thwarted mining company profits and independence. It was in this action that the pattern for success for Kaiser Wilhelm was first seen. Through social constructs of welfare systems and protections, the Kaiser would further erode the Chancellor's office and expand his own influence in German society.

The Kaiser attempted to expand the social policies further in widespread fashion, opening the government's treasuries to revolutionary new social constructs. Bismarck opposed the new laws and legislation coming from the Kaiser including increasing wages, improving working conditions and regulating labor relations. Bismarck was convinced that an expansion of the social systems of Germany would bankrupt the country, and he began to publicly denounce the changes to German society.

In fact, Bismarck began to institute a series of new laws in order to stop the expansion of Socialism in pre-World War I Germany. By early 1890 Bismarck was sponsoring widespread anti-socialist laws to stop the spreading strikes by labor leaders who demanded more from the government, and who had now tasted the benefits of a monarch favorable to their cause, as well as generous payments and entitlements from the treasury.

The Kaiser became increasingly involved in the social order of German society, especially the treatment of mine workers who went on strike in 1890. Following his policy of active participation in government, he routinely interrupted Bismarck in Council to make clear where he stood on social policy. Bismarck sharply disagreed with Wilhelm's policy and worked to circumvent it. Even though Wilhelm supported the altered anti-Socialist bill, Bismarck pushed for his support to veto the bill in its entirety, but when Bismarck's arguments could not convince Wilhelm, he became excited and agitated until uncharacteristically he blurted out his motive for having the bill fail--he wanted the Socialists to agitate until a violent clash occurred that could be used as a pretext to crush them. Wilhelm replied

---

that he was not willing to open his reign with a bloody campaign against his subjects.

And so the social expansions continued until finally the conflict between Bismarck and the Kaiser came to a head in 1895 with the Kaiser sponsoring a "Labor Conference" in Berlin where the Kaiser would finally cement his power and isolate the civilian government under Bismarck. The conference opened in May of 1895, and the Kaiser stated that the most pressing issue was the further enlargement of the bill concerning the protection of the laborer. Finally the Reichstag had passed a series of Workers Protection Acts which improved working conditions, protected women and children and regulated labor relations. The people rejoiced, or at least the powerful blocs of the labor unions did. Bismarck was undone and dismissed from his post.

The Royal families of the Habsburg and Hohenzollern dynasties were now firmly in control of one third of Europe and stood to restore a more feudal order of society with the social constructs of labor and wage controls in the hands of the crown. Kaiser Wilhelm had simply opened the treasuries to direct entitlements to the population and expanded the generosity of the German government to the point of bankruptcy in order to accomplish the most sweeping change of government policy in Germany since the rise of German autonomy.

However, the Kaiser's militaristic and expansionist foreign policy stood in direct contradiction to his socialistic domestic policy. Wilhelm greatly expanded the role of the military in the period from 1890-1900 building a Navy that would attempt to challenge the British naval power, and he expanded the use of their underwater fleet with unrestricted piracy on the high seas. This great dichotomy between social policy and an aggressive military became emblematic of German government development until the fall of the Third Reich in 1945.

The important thing to note is that this expansion of military imperialism, the control of the population through social services, and the seizure of properties and business through social systems is ultimately a rethinking of the feudalism and militarism of his Royal predecessors. Wilhelm was remodeling a monarchical society from a 20th century viewpoint with astounding success--at least for the time being. Society was once again being planned from the top down with little to no input from purely private interests.

The return to feudal autocracy and its subsequent brutality of the peasants by the ruling class of barons and dukes did not take long under Wilhelm. A well published incident where the Baron Clement von Kettner brutally beat a Chinese boy and then murdered him by shooting him to death, led to a massive response by the Chinese in the area, and von Kettner was then murdered in turn by General Dong Fuxiang during the Boxer Rebellion of 1900. The Kaiser's view on the matter was quintessentially Royal in nature, and speaks volumes about the attitude of the Kaiser:

*Should you encounter the enemy, he will be defeated! No quarter will be given! Prisoners will not be taken! Whoever falls into your hands is forfeited. Just as a thousand years ago the Huns under their King Attila made a name for themselves, one that even today makes them seem mighty in history and legend, may the name German be affirmed by you in such a way in China that no Chinese will ever again dare to look cross-eyed at a German* (Kaiser Wilhlem, 1900).

This speech, made by the Kaiser at the outset of the Boxer rebellion was attributed primarily to Asian indifference and racial prejudice against people of color. Although some of that may have been true, there is no doubt that the real power of the speech lay in the authority of the monarchy. The speech could just as easily been attributed to a king from the Holy Roman empire against the Muslims, or the English crown about the Scottish.

The Boxer Rebellion, and the moves by the Kaiser which eventually led to World War I, nevertheless did not move the Kaiser away from his favoritism of social change in Germany and his understanding that liberal and socialist restructuring was the key to rebuilding feudal and monarchical government in Europe, no matter the outcome of the wars. Finally in 1917, during the war with the French, his aggressive promotion of social restructuring in Germany moved the

Bolsheviks[24] to attack the Russian Tsars and break their power. The action of the German entitlements was motivating the Russian people as the American Revolution moved the French people against their government in the 1790's. The Kaiser was not blind to the reverse parallel, and the Kaiser wanted the powerful Tsars broken--that was clear. The war with France in the West was going badly for Wilhelm, and an alliance with the Russians under the Bolsheviks, which had so far eluded him, could provide the tipping power.

When the Bolsheviks failed in their first attempt to do away with the Tsars, the Kaiser provided sanctuary and passage for Lenin. He provided that aid to Lenin and the failing revolution for a variety of reasons, one of which was that he thought Lenin would provide aid to him on his failing Western Front should he win in Russia by ending the war on the Eastern Front. Had the Kaiser

---

[24] The Bolsheviks, founded by Vladimir Lenin, were by 1905 a mass organization consisting primarily of workers under a democratic internal hierarchy governed by the principle of democratic centralism who considered themselves the leaders of the revolutionary working class of Russia. Their beliefs and practices were often referred to as Bolshevism. Bolshevik revolutionary leader Leon Trotsky commonly used the terms "Bolshevism" and "Bolshevist" after his exile from the Soviet Union to differentiate between what he saw as true Leninism and the regime within the state and the party which arose under Stalin.- *Bolshevism, the Road to Revolution*, by Alan Woods.

---

not provided this aid and ability for Lenin to sneak back into Russia, it is likely the Communist Revolution would not have succeeded[25].

The irony of the affair was of course, that the Kaiser was now making war against another royal family, one that was firmly entrenched in power, and he could not have foreseen that his foment of rebellion in Russia would backfire against him terribly. The Communists, although a bud from the trees of Socialism that Wilhelm had planted in 1890 in Germany, were now virulently anti- royal and saw themselves as true rescuers of common labor rights viewing the Royals as an obstacle all along.

By 1918, with the war going badly and draining the Kaisers coffers, he could no longer afford the massive social constructs he had created 20 years earlier, and the labor movements that he so carefully cultivated now moved against him and he was forced to abdicate his position. With the Russians no longer having any taste for

---

[25] The Bolsheviks decided to make peace immediately with the German Empire to please the Russian people prior to the Revolution. Vladimir Lenin's political enemies attributed this decision to his aid by the foreign office of Wilhelm II, German Emperor. This was further bolstered by the German Foreign Ministry's sponsorship of Lenin's return to Petrograd.

---

war, as the new government under Lenin was essentially bankrupt, the wars in Europe ended, and the Kaiser now lived in exile.

But royal money and power was never really gone, and the Germans certainly were not the bloodthirsty Bolsheviks, and they allowed the Kaiser and his royal family to live in a castle in Huis Doorn in the Netherlands. Involving himself in non-political affairs and with a great love of archeology, Wilhelm (he lost the title of Kaiser but retained his personal royal titles) simply faded into the background and let the newly legitimized German Republic under Adolf Hitler flourish.

After the brutal suffering of the German people for years under the yoke of the war reparations of the Western powers, it was only natural that an Adolf Hitler could rise to power and take advantage of the same social order theory that Wilhelm had established. The Nazi's National Socialist Party established their authority in the same way Wilhelm had, through reconstruction of the state as a mechanism of the distribution of wealth. The Nazi's were socialists, at least at first. They reestablished many of the rights and benefits of the labor movement, revoked the rights of weapon ownership and established a firm hold of government over the day to day freedoms of the people.[26]

Wilhelm, although determined not to make his feelings public about the growing Nazi movement, was resolute in his support of Hitler. In the wake of the German victory over Poland in September 1939, Wilhelm's adjutant, General von Dommes, wrote on his behalf to Hitler stating that the House of Hohenzollern "remained loyal" and noted that nine Prussian Princes (one son and eight grandchildren) were stationed at the front, concluding:

*Because of the special circumstances that require residence in a neutral foreign country, His Majesty must personally decline to make the aforementioned comment. The Emperor has therefore charged me with making a communication* (General von Dommes, October 1939).

---

[26] The Nazis accused Communism and capitalism of being associated with Jewish influences and interests. They declared support for a nationalist form of Socialism that was to provide for the Aryan race and the German nation: economic security, social welfare programs for workers, a just wage, honor for workers' importance to the nation, and protection from capitalist exploitation.

---

Wilhelm stayed in regular contact with Hitler through General von Dommes who represented the family in Germany. There was also no question later on of Wilhelm's feelings on the matter of German supremacy in Europe. He also felt that many of the royal families had been contaminated with Jewish blood, and Wilhelm may have helped to lay the foundation for the growing anti-Semitism in pre-World War II Germany:

> *Freemasons thoroughly infected by Juda... and the British people must be liberated from Antichrist Juda. We must drive Juda out of England just as he has been chased out of the Continent* (Kaiser Wilhelm II, 1941).

Critical to this line of thought was Wilhelm's false belief that English Freemasons and Jews had caused the two World Wars, aiming at a world Jewish empire with England and funded by American gold. He also foresaw a unified Europe under German rule claiming that the result of World War II would be a "U.S. of

Europe!" In a letter to his sister Princess Margaret in 1940, Wilhelm wrote:

> *The hand of God is creating a new world & working miracles ... We are becoming the U.S. of Europe under German leadership, a united European Continent.....the Jews* [are] *being thrust out of their nefarious positions in all countries, whom they have driven to hostility for centuries.*

This anti-Semitic feeling was fuel on the fire of Hitler's crusade against the Jews in Germany and possibly was a catalyst in the persecution and extermination of Jews in World War II Germany. Although Hitler, who was anti-monarchy, disliked Wilhelm both privately and publicly, Wilhelm (1940) sent a telegram to Hitler upon his successes stating, "Congratulations, you have won using my troops."

After the Nazi conquest of the Netherlands in 1940, the aging Wilhelm retired completely from public life. His health was failing, as well as his wealth, and subsidies from the German government had now all but ceased. It is hard to say whether Wilhelm influenced Hitler, or the reverse was true--Hitler was strongly anti-royal in his sentiments. It is also possible that the wave of anti-Semitic hysteria that swept Germany at the time was simply a product of narrow minded racism in the face of ever increasing economic distress and the strong nationalist movement under Hitler's Third Reich. The mechanics of the Final Solution are well documented, but the original fomentation and spread of its racism may never be known. Wilhelm, nearing death and learning about Hitler's Final Solution, wrote: "For the first time, I am ashamed to be a German."

The historical failure of Hitler and the Third Reich is well known and well documented, and bears no repeating, but the labor movement and social constructs of both Wilhelm and the early Nazi Party remain. Another period of unfettered Capitalism and the expansion of post-war European economies after decimation a second time from two World Wars, meant the Royals would have to postpone their return to power for some time. During the 1950's and 1960's, under the split government of East and West Germany, the Royals bided their time and waited knowing full well that the social labor movements would be essential to their future once the Americans and Russians fled Europe for other more pressing matters. The key to that success meant breaking the back of the explosion of Capitalism in post-World War II Europe. The effects of Germany's breakup and collapse under Nazism and the Second World War were catastrophic to the power of many Royal families, and blame began to shift toward Wilhelm's activities during the First World War as a precursor to the Second. In England the king's abdication sent further shock waves around the world.

With the Royals out of the spotlight, a great calm in government and politics settled over the world. The average citizen of not only Germany but the world was weary from two cataclysmically violent wars, and the taste of power and wealth was now bitter with the blood of the dead. It was the United States that came out on top, both economically and militarily, and with its sole possession of atomic weaponry. Peace at last had settled in Europe even if tensions between the now communist Russia (USSR) and the United States were at an all time high.

However, just as it was after the Napoleonic wars, peace would be fleeting. The Royals would use this socialist blueprint again. They would attempt to repeat the successes of Wilhelm and his near miss at recapturing the world, even if it meant the possibility of risking another Adolf Hitler.

# The Nuclear Battlefield

*Prince Georg Friedrich in Vanity Fair September 2003: "The people of Germany should start thinking about bringing back the monarchy... in fact I am sure it will happen."*
*-Georg Friedrich, Prince of Prussia*

With Russia's control of Eastern German provinces and the Baltic states the focus on Germany as the predominant central European power had come to a screeching halt. It would be 50 years before the country would be unified again, and in those years the country remained a pawn between the power politics of the two giant powers of the West and the East. Germany was merely another target on the now atomic battlefield.

As time passed Germans began to wonder, sometimes loudly, about the wisdom of keeping Western troops stationed in their country to protect it from Soviet occupation. Various political movements sprang up to voice their opposition to being a pawn in the twin superpowers Cold War struggle. The common German view was that there could only be one outcome--a decimated Germany with mushroom-shaped clouds. Because fundamentally and politically they could not oust American and British troops from Germany, the target quickly developed into one against atomic energy itself. Atomic weapons and power were seen, perhaps incorrectly, as a villain in the high stakes game of world domination. The Cold War, at least for the Germans, was a war about nuclear fission and its uses not one of political or governmental ideology. Thus environmental politics and socialist theory once again found fertile ground in the German people under the closing vice of American occupation and Soviet expansionism.

Green politics is the byword for today's movement toward strict government controls on industrialization and its subsequent damaging effects on the environment. The movement toward a more green society began in Germany in the late 1970's, and since then green political parties have developed in many countries across the globe most recently in the United States.

The political term Green, a translation of the German Grün, was coined by *die Grunen*, a Green Party formed in the late 1970's in Germany. *Die Grunen* established a fundamental precept of opposition to nuclear power and industrialization and opposition to NATO[27] (North Atlantic Treaty Organization) and its members military defense of Europe. It is this last platform piece that is the key to understanding the current aim of Green politics[28].

In the 1970's, faced with an increasing nuclear threat from Communism, NATO was formed to act as a military deterrent and barrier to the USSR regarding Communist expansion in Europe. The Royals realized too that as long as NATO had its armies parked all over Europe any hope of a return to a feudal government

---

[27] The North Atlantic Treaty Organization or NATO, also called the North Atlantic Alliance, is an intergovernmental military alliance based on the North Atlantic Treaty which was signed on 4, April, 1949. The NATO headquarters are in Brussels, Belgium, and the organization constitutes a system of collective defense whereby its member states agree to mutual defense in response to an attack by any external party.

[28] The Green Party of the United States (GPUS), not to be confused with the German Greens, is a voluntary association of state green parties and has been active as a nationally recognized political party since 2001. Prior to national formation, many state affiliates had already formed and were recognized by other state parties. The Association of State Green Parties (ASGP), a forerunner organization, first gained widespread public attention during Ralph Nader's presidential runs in 1996 and 2000. With the founding of the Green Party of the United States, a national political presence was established. GPUS became the primary national Green organization in the United States eclipsing the earlier Greens/Green Party USA.

---

would necessarily fail regardless of how much funding and effort was put into restoring the monarchy. The Kaiser's military adventures had ingrained itself in the collective Royal thought.

The Green Movement's foundation stood against America and her allies and was a pro-Soviet political party both funded and designed to thwart NATO protections. Since NATO's funding came primarily from America and capitalistic ventures, in order to bring down NATO or at least act as a stumbling block, the Green Party sought to bring down capitalism as a driving economic force. To topple the gigantic power of NATO, the theory was to destroy its funding first.

The Green Movement certainly had friends in post-Bolshevik Soviet Russia. They too stood to benefit from a collapse of NATO. The remaining Soviets, who also were teetering on bankruptcy, still remembered the years of Wilhelm supporting Lenin against the Tsars. A socialistic Germany along with an expulsion of NATO meant the possibility of a massive expansion of the Russian economy and perhaps its own borders into Germany. This was particularly critical to Russia to slow the advance of NATO since its own economy had been crippled by the war with Germany. They needed time to catch up.

What better way to accomplish the goal than limit its consumption of resources, drive its costs of manufacturing goods up, and deter the natural forces of economic expansion through negative publicity? The best way to build a new socially-ordered society with monarchical rule was to break down the old order and freedoms much as the Kaiser did in World War I.

Unfortunately most of the Kaiser's children were wiped out by scandal, accident and war. The family was in disrepair post-1945, and much of their wealth was depleted. However, the youngest of the Kaiser's children, Victoria Louise had married the Duke of Brunswick, an eminently wealthy Royal. The Duke abdicated his kingdom to the Weimar Republic in exchange for retaining his wealth[29]. As a result their children and heirs stood to gain immeasurably through the elimination of the American occupation of Germany and the expulsion of NATO.

---

[29] Only in 1913 was peace sealed with the marriage of Prince Ernest Augustus of Hanover to Victoria Louise, daughter of the German emperor William II. This couple was enthroned in the duchy of Brunswick. To this day the princes of Hanover also are titled Prince(s) of Great Britain and Ireland, Duke of Brunswick and Lüneburg.

You can get an indication of where today's Green politics comes from by looking at some of the movements of its early founders. Take for instance the case of Joseph Martin "Joschka" Fischer who is one of the key figures and principal founders of the German Green Party. Fischer was a student of Marx, Mao and Hegel, and was a member of the militant group *Revolutionärer Kampf* (Revolutionary Struggle). The 1970's was a period of student activism and of German Green Party struggles. During that time Fischer became a leader to the radical Greens and engaged in violent actions against the German police. Photos of one such battle in March, 1973 show him clubbing policeman Rainer Marx to whom he later publicly apologized.

The actions of Fischer, and their relation to modern Green politics, are not unique. Many of the Green Party's other founders, such as Daniel Cohn-Bendit, a close friend of Fischer and Herbert Gruhl, are all are connected with violent protest actions at their earliest days. Although those violent actions have now been denounced by their leaders, and have characterized the Green Movement as non-violent--at the party's core is the bubbling turmoil of anti-capitalistic fervor. The key

—

point in the shift of the German Green Party from a violent anti-NATO group to a modern day political powerhouse did not happen until the mid-1980's. Backed by heavy funding from a variety of left wing groups and interests, they gained significant momentum by winning elections in the German Bundestag. This was a significant event as it marked the first time green politicos were able to win seats in a national election and have influence in a modern European government. After that election the Green Party's power grew substantially. It was aided by the moves of NATO to increase unpopular nuclear weapons for defense, and the Chernobyl crisis of 1986. The public began to take notice of the effects of the widespread use of nuclear power, and their growing fear of expansion led to the wider popularity of the Green Party influence in German. There was widespread expansion of influence into other European countries, such as England, France and Finland

This German Green Party influence would have substantial and profound changes to the largely capitalistic economies of Europe in the 1980's. Green Party politics stand against conventional Capitalism and emphasizes economic growth while ignoring ecological health which is anathema to green politics. Green politics considers such growth to be "uneconomic" growth and view such material increases that nonetheless lowers overall quality of life *vis a vis* a return to a simpler lifestyle.

As we look back to the eventual fall of feudalistic economies and the demise of monarchical power, one can see why many of the decimated royal houses of Europe would support such growth in green power. One of the key components of green policy is the concept of bioregionalism: the theory that political, cultural and environmental boundaries are based on naturally-defined areas called bioregions or ecoregions. Bioregions are defined through physical and environmental features including soil and terrain characteristics and watershed boundaries[30]. Bioregionalism stresses that the determination of a bioregion emphasizes the local

---

[30] The term appears to have originated in work by Peter Berg and Raymond Dasmann in the early 1970s. This view opposes a homogeneous economy and consumer culture with its lack of stewardship towards the environment. Some of its tenets include but are not limited to: Ensuring that political boundaries match ecological boundaries, highlight the unique ecology of the bioregion, encourage consumption of local foods where possible, encourage the use of local materials where possible, encourage the cultivation of native plants of the region, and encourage sustainability in harmony with the bioregion.

---

monarch's knowledge and solutions as opposed to external forces. Local order and governance is central to feudalism. Remember, a king runs his lands via local control of resources through his landowners or barons. Thus the Green Movement and its political goal to break capitalism fits with the restoration of the monarchy's power, and feudalism.

It also allows for monarchical authority to still benefit from the incredible growth potential of capitalism. This governmental authority could subsequently be controlled by the heads of the Royal families and they could profit from it. This is important, since Royal wealth is from heredity entitlement and is essentially isolated from the rest of the European economies.

Consider another leg of the green political movement--Social Progressivism[31]. The precepts of

---

[31] Social progressives in the United States are associated with the left wing of the Democratic Party. The Congressional Progressive Caucus in the United States House of Representatives works together to advance liberal issues and positions. The group advocates "universal access to affordable, high quality healthcare," fair trade agreements, living wage laws, right of workers to organize, abolition of significant portions of the USA PATRIOT Act, legalization of same-sex marriage, campaign finance reform laws, a complete pullout from the war in Iraq, a crackdown on corporate welfare and influence, an increase in income tax rates for the upper class, a decrease in income tax rates for the lower class, and an increase in welfare spending by the federal government.

---

Social Progressivism tout that science and secular philosophy have no true value in society. They believe that the social constructs[32] of family, monogamous marriage and gender identity are not fundamental to a well-ordered society and that social change is deemed to be for the greater good of society. feudalism also holds that a well-ordered society can only be established through non-traditional social constructs and a more pastoral lifestyle--a lifestyle that relies heavily on village social constructs governed by a monarchical fiefdom. This sort of lifestyle and social order is heavily dependent on manorial or monarchical governance, where land carries the obligation that the peasant's household supplies the lord with specified labor services or a part of its output (or cash in the form of taxation).

When examining the concept of household supply and labor services in exchange for output, one can better understand the modern day construct of Socialism and why modern royal houses have endorsed the green

---

[32] Social construction (social construct) is a concept or practice that is the construct (or artifact) of a particular group. When we say that something is socially constructed, we are focusing on its dependence on contingent variables of our social selves rather than any inherent quality that it possesses in itself.

political movement. Central to green theory is the movement of resources as controlled by government in exchange for a portion of the goods produced from those resources. Current European retirement social constructs derive their monies from the seizure of a portion of the populations output in the form of taxes, but do so in manner that exceeds the actual personal profit. In short, the government makes more than earner. If government were also to control the flow of resources into the system as well as the resultant output in the form of taxes, a government could have total control over a normally free and capitalistic economy even while its workers believe they are in a free economy. This illusion of freedom would naturally benefit a monarchical and feudal lifestyle looking to avoid the previous failures that led to two World Wars under Kaiser Wilhelm.

Much like early feudalism, Green politics would restore power to a centralized authority and an unequal application of law. Fundamental to any orderly society is the establishment and equal application of laws. One of the main precepts that define a society is its application of the law and its consequences. Take the case of Nazi Germany and its anti-Jewish laws. Nazism defined that period in German history- to its detriment, and eventually the men that instituted those laws were found to be guilty of the worst crimes a leader can commit, the unequal application of its laws, and how it allowed millions to be slaughtered. Had the Nazi applied the law equally to all, the mass exterminations in concentration camps would have been near impossible, as Jews would have had the same rights as any other citizen. From the code of Hammurabi to the law books written today, the equal application of the law is central to good societal management.

Green politics does not have as its fundamental core an equal application of laws. It applies law unequally based on an arbitrary set of rules set up by the keepers of the environment--the government or monarch. Thus with the control of the economy firmly in the hands of the state, it sets up a system that would be ripe for abuse even if handled in a benevolent and non-obtrusive manner at the outset. Eventually the whims of government officials and the agenda of an individual or set of individuals would determine economic output and who would and would not benefit.

The restoration of Royal power in control of centralized and socialistic government however, is a bit trickier affair. Money is power, particularly in a modern European government, and the biggest obstacle to the Royal domination of European economies is the flow of capital from one economy to another. For monarchical control to return, the Royal families would have to break the European currencies, which would be no easy affair. The ever changing value of the German mark, the French lira, and the Italian lire, make expansion and control of their economies a problematic affair. If one managed to control German industrial power, it could easily convert to French lira and reinvent its value in another country. It would be like squeezing a soap bubble. Grab the economy in Germany it would squirt over to France, and then perhaps to Spain or Ireland, as each currency competed for the tax dollars.

Thus the concept of the Euro was born and you begin to see the light as to why the Royals helped to fund the Green political power movement and drive to a European Union that had now gotten a foothold in Germany in the 1980's. Green Party theories, now with a sizeable beachhead in the German government, began to make treatises and pounded the drum to a more equalized European trade union. There were serious problems in the early 1980's in the European trade markets due mostly to Asian influences, chiefly the influx of cheap goods made in the Pacific markets which were rapidly diminishing the ability of European markets to compete. Thus there was a movement to make Europe more competitive by reworking the Treaty of 1957[33]. A commission was formed to develop a unified European trading bloc, and at its head was liberal socialist Jacque Delors[34].

Jacque Delors, conveniently was a man who all along had ties with the old Royal monies and the labor

---

[33] The European Economic Community (EEC) (also known as the Common Market in the English-speaking world, renamed the European Community (EC) in 1993) was an international organization created with a view to bring about economic integration (including a single market) among the Inner Six of European integration; the Western European countries of Belgium, France, Germany, Italy, Luxembourg and the Netherlands.The EEC was created by the Treaty establishing the European Economic Community (Treaty of Rome; renamed Treaty on the functioning of the European Union in 2009) of 1957.

[34] In 1974, Delors joined the French Socialist Party, with other left-wing Christians. He was one of the rare members of the party to be openly religious, thus challenging its long-standing secular tradition. He served in the European Parliament from 1979 to 1981.Under President François Mitterrand, Delors served as Economics and Finance Minister from 1981–1983, and Economics, Finance, and Budget Minister from 1983–1984. He advocated a pause in the social policies, a clear acceptance of the market economy and an alignment with European social democracy.

movements of the 1970's, and owed a significant amount of his life's success to them[35]. It was a debt they would call in, at the Delors Commission as the newly appointed chief of the European Union.

To say that the Delors Commission and Jacque Delors was the chief architect of a European union is an understatement. Without Delors there most likely would *not* be an EU as we know it today. The Delors Report issued from the Commission not only established the EU as a solid unified trading bloc, it also recommended and worked toward the establishment of a single European currency- the Euro. The Delors commission worked tirelessly toward a single goal--the unification of Europe as a single economic trading partner and the development of a single European currency.

Faced with growing economic stagnation, the concept of a single powerful trading bloc appealed to most Europeans. But Europe neglected to acknowledge the chief reason for the growing stagnation which was the combination of Asian influence amplified by the expansion of regulation and governance by Green

---

[35]In the 1940s–1960s, Delors held a series of posts in French banking and state planning with the Royal Banque de France.

policies. They focused instead on unifying currencies and removing inter-European trade barriers, which while helpful in the short run, would only serve to later increase the pain.

But it was those trade barriers and currency differentiations that actually protected Capitalism and economic expansion. Fluctuating currencies and the varying values of goods could be more easily managed and provided a firewall against economic failure. Should Italy go bankrupt, the other European trading partners could bail them out with their own more stable currencies. Using a single currency such as the Euro and by having unified trade position, those protections would go away. If Spain or France were to economically collapse it could theoretically destroy the more substantial economies of Germany or England--a goal that Green politicians have sought for years. Wilhelm's dream of a "U.S. of Europe" was coming to fruition. Cutting off the economic protections of Europe would potentially bring an earlier demise to NATO and capitalistic expansion.

The use of NATO as an environmental scapegoat to further Green politics was a viable one and gained traction as stories of NATO practice bombings and atomic testing became widespread. As the fuel grew so did the fire and NATO became the primary enemy to the environment. Progressives and leftist groups flocked to the cause, and money poured into the Green Party coffers well into the 1990's.

It didn't hurt that there was a worldwide boom driven by expansion in the United States economy and the plentiful supply of Asian labor, making goods inexpensive to purchase and money cheap. The Green Party in Germany retooled the economy, and the country was ripe for reintegration. The weaknesses in the Soviet economy were bringing the downfall of the old Communist government. The Berlin wall came down, and Germany was a nation again. This put even more pressure on NATO which was now seen as a relic of World War II.

However, the Green Party in Germany had built its reputation on blame. By 1995, with the economy solid and Germany becoming an economic stronghold in Europe, Germans began to question the wisdom of politics driven by environmentalist industrial strangulation. Although today the Green Party still is an integral part of German society, compromises have been made with opposing viewpoints in order to maintain and consolidate their power.

A coalition government between leftist Green leaders and more conservative elements is in charge today, and although Germany still maintains a high level of Green theory in its societal planning, changes are beginning to be seen at almost every level. The theory that companies are inherently damaging is no longer central to German political theory, and NATO is a mere ghost of what it was only 25 years ago. Although NATO still represents 70% of the world's defense spending, the Berlin Accords of 2002 allow the EU to draw on NATO as its own tactical reserve of defenses, easing the monetary burden on socialized governments and as a result no NATO is no longer viewed as a "first strike force." NATO is now used more and more in peacekeeping operations rather than as a true military bulwark against Russian aggression.

It would be a misnomer to characterize the Green Movement as a direct instrument of the royal families attempt to regain power. Rather the Green Party and green politics in general have many of the same goals that the Royals have, and by funding, promoting and inserting themselves into the structure of the Green Movement they are becoming one and the same. Whatever bodes well for Green politics bodes well for the Royals. And it is important to note that the Royals and their families are not as concerned with the passing of time as they are an enormously patient political force due to the nature of inherited wealth and power. If the baron does not accomplish what needs to be done in his lifetime, then that duty then passes to the son.

It comes with the territory of generational power and wealth, and the contemplation of eternity.

# HRH Charles of the Garden

*Something as curious as the monarchy won't survive unless you take account of people's attitudes. After all, if people don't want it, they won't have it.-Prince Charles*

There is an old saying--follow the money. Modern day (post-1970) green issues are a favorite of the English crown. Prince Charles has been a valuable fundraiser for green issues. In September of 2010, Charles spent several weeks travelling about England in his royal train promoting the concepts of green living including cycling and biofuels. His 2009 book *"Harmony"* is a best seller, and the politics of the book speak volumes on the Royal's position of ecological reform and its intended damage to capitalistic endeavors.

One of the principal arguments in Prince Charles' book and his politics is a return to organic farming instead of large industrial farming which has been astonishingly successful in feeding the world for the past 300 years. Prince Charles on localized farming:

*I believe that true sustainability depends fundamentally upon us shifting our perception and widening our focus, so that we understand, again, that we have a sacred duty of stewardship of the natural order of things... If we could rediscover that sense of harmony; that sense of being a part of, rather than apart from nature, we would perhaps be less likely to see the world as some sort of gigantic production system, capable of ever-increasing outputs for our benefit – at no cost* (Prince Charles, 2009).

In other words, the expansion of economic and capitalistic interests stands in direct opposition to "economic harmony" with the environment. Charles has made his position plain; Capitalism is a threat to our long- term survival and he stands in opposition to it. Most importantly, he ignores the fact that without modern agricultural techniques in place today, food pricing would be far more expensive and widespread availability of cheap foodstuffs would be unheard of. Naturally, a large scale return to organic and non-industrial farming would increase worldwide food pricing and destabilize world governments -perhaps irreparably.

According to the New York Times[36], Charles has used his influence in royal circles to quash other pro-Capitalistic endeavors in addition to funding green politics. Take for example the move by England's Lord Rogers to develop 13 acres in Chelsea with 500-plus new apartments in the modernist style, as well as a sports center, a community center and a hotel. Prince Charles thought the plan was "unsympathetic" and "unsuitable," and would clash with the architecture of the area-- particularly the Royal Hospital across the street designed by Christopher Wren. He said so in a letter to the site's owner, a development company controlled by the Qatari royal family. Just before the project was expected to be approved by local planners who had worked out its kinks in some 80 meetings with Lord Rogers's firm--the development company, Qatar Diar, announced it would not be employing Lord Rogers or using his plans at all. The influence of the English crown was keenly felt by Rogers.

---

[36] *Prince Charles Defends His Involvement in Architecture Dispute-NYT* Dave Itzkoff, 6/30/2010.

Charles' involvement in architecture has also attracted controversy, especially his personal intervention to redesign projects whose architectural style or approach he has opposed. He has been especially opposed to styles such as modernism and functionalism. Richard Rogers, recipient of the Pritzker Prize and Stirling Prize, has described the Prince's personal intervention in projects as "an abuse of power" and "unconstitutional[37]." This sort of activist architectural intervention shows the influence of Charles on the school of modernist thought and English society.

Charles has moved into the realm of environmental theory as well. By his own account, Charles' charitable influence runs over $10 million a year. Charles' activities are not limited by stymieing economic development either. He has also been active in developing "eco-friendly" clothing lines and other consumer goods[38].

---

[37] Booth, Robert (June 15th, 2009). "Prince Charles's meddling in planning 'unconstitutional', says Richard Rogers". The Guardian (London).

[38] *Prince Charles Tells Us to Get Woolly Again*-by Bonnie Alter, London 2/18/2010.

The links between the Green Movement's goals and the Royal's goals, are not limited to the English crown's donations. Not by a long shot. The English have always maintained a tradition of "gardening" politics in the sense that they are keenly aware of the effects of environmental policy on their lives. England is an island with limited resources and limited opportunities for expansion. It has been an historical fact that many of England's wars against her neighbors were the result of the English crown looking for more lands and resources to tax and profit from. As a result the English economy has been very reliant on environmental conditions and the effects of industry upon it.

The effects of mechanization have been profound on English industry. Child labor was substantially on the rise as the need for cheap labor increased. Crowding from the influx of labor led to high crime and poor living conditions in the mid-1800's as factories expanded to accommodate the influx of cheap resources and massive growth of the English economy. The expansion of English industrialization was not all negative because that massive growth in the economy led to enormous public improvements in infrastructure in order to handle the masses. The Tube was built in 1863 and the London Bridge in 1894 as well as famous public areas such as Trafalgar Square, Royal Albert Hall and the Big Ben--all of which are now trademarks of London and in turn England herself.

In comparison to today's more socialistic government which has produced only limited growth in public facilities and the economy, the expansion of 1800's England was mind-bogglingly swift. Ironically, it was this expansionist period of the English industrialization that also saw the furthest erosion of English power in the world; a fact not lost on the Royal houses of Europe. As the freedoms and wealth of the English citizenry increased, the power and influence of the Royals waned. It was under Queen Victoria's England that the transition from a feudal monarchy to a constitutional[39] one was completed. Although England saw the greatest expansion of its territorial influence

---

[39] A constitutional monarchy is a form of government in which a monarch acts as head of state within the parameters of a constitution, whether it be a written, uncodified or blended constitution. This form of government differs from absolute monarchy in that an absolute monarch serves as the sole source of political power in the state and is not legally bound by any constitution- *What is constitutional monarchy?"*. Official website of the British Monarchy.

during this period, it also saw its greatest decline of royal power.

The transition of a monarchical power to a more secular government was a transition that few noticed tried to stop. Even Queen Victoria, following the death of her husband in 1861, had become more and more reclusive. Since a female monarch could not directly pass her lineage onto another house for royal transition of power, it unavoidably weakened the House of Hanover[40] and led to the rise of the House of Windsor (the current monarchy). Thus when the greatest threat to England, in the form of German nationalist supremacy by Wilhelm and Hitler finally arrived, it was the secular government that was best able to protect the people--not the royal houses. It was only natural that English citizens began to question the necessity of a monarchy at all.

As the call from the people to dethrone the monarchs of England grew steam, the Royal houses of England increased their support of the Green Movement and green politics in Europe. Since early adulthood,

---

[40] The House of Hanover (the Hanoverians) is a German royal dynasty which has ruled the Duchy of Brunswick-Lüneburg (German: *Braunschweig-Lüneburg*), the Kingdom of Hanover and the Kingdom of Great Britain and the Kingdom of Ireland.

Prince Charles has become gradually more involved in the theoretical concept of managing the economy directly rather than a free capitalistic economy and he did it through support of the more radical elements of green political theory[41]. Charles' support for the more radical elements of anti-Capitalistic theory was evident in a speaking engagement at the Oxford University in 2010 as well. Princes Charles urged the world to follow Islamic spiritual principles in order to save the environment. In a high profile speech, the heir to the throne argued that man's destruction of the world was contrary to the scriptures of all religions--but particularly that of the Islamic faith.[42] Charles said:

*The inconvenient truth[43] is that we share this planet with the rest of creation for a very good reason--and that is, we cannot exist on our own without the intricately balanced web of life*

---

[41] *Prince Charles of Arabia* by Ronni L. Gordon and David M. Stillman-Middle East Quarterly

[42] *Prince Charles: Defender of the (Islamic) Faith* June 9, 2010- G. Brock

[43] Note his use of the expression 'inconvenient truth', the title of Al Gore's bible on environmentalism.

*around us... Islam has always taught this and to ignore that lesson is to default on our contract with creation.*

This evolution of environmental protectionism through economic control and supporting the radical Islamic fundamentalist movement is nothing new to those that follow Progressive politics. In the same way Wilhelm defended Nazism and Communism to the German people in order to garner favor and political power, Charles is also using the anti-capitalistic concept of Islamic extremism to further his own ends. Nazis had supported Islamic terrorist groups through World War II in an effort to counter Jewish growth and British influence in the Middle East. The current Muslim Brotherhood had its roots in anti-Semitic principles and trained under Nazi instructors. Although there is no doubt that the current Muslim Brotherhood is not a Nazi puppet, its fundamental theory is based on anti-Semitic politics and pro-Jihadist policies[44].

---

[44] *Today's Muslim Brotherhood Grew Out of World War II Era Nazi Eugenics Doctrines*- CK Hunter 02/07/2011.

The organization and establishment of the current English monarchies, charities and trusts is a rather complex maze with Charles as the titular or direct head of most of them. Upon cursory examination, Charles is involved with many notable charitable affairs that promote job creation for underprivileged and troubled youths, the protection of historic buildings as well his considerable development of Green charities that protect the environment. However, there seems to be a common thread linking all of them which follows his own line of thought both in speech and writing--that we must not progress forward as a culture and that we must not go too far from the traditional roots of feudalistic society.

Prince Charles' charities and architectural committees involving the protection of historical buildings in England are fairly extensive. They go much further than the simple preservation of historic architecture in cities. They have taken an activist approach to the prevention of "new" or "modernist" architecture in England. This also means limits in the growth of the construction and building of new facilities that do not meet with the committee's standards. Using these forums, Charles has continued to put forward his views stressing traditional urbanism as a need for human beings and the restoration of historic buildings as an integrated element of new development and sustainable design. Thus his charity takes an almost activist approach to construction, and strives to collapse modernism and progress in an effort to lock people into not forgetting their past. It is a subtle, but hardly gentle, reminder that people should not move forward but rather move backward toward monarchical rule.

Indications are that Charles' personal interest in the environment became more pronounced after his move to the Highgrove Estate in 1980. Over the years Charles has remade the estate into a more environmentally sensitive land tract. From the Highgrove website:

> *A specially built reed bed sewage system, much loved by dragonflies at its treatment end, is used for all Highgrove's waste. Rare trees and plants are planted for future generations to enjoy and heritage seeds are planted in areas to keep the varieties going.... This ethically sound management is carried through to the house too, where bottles and cans are recycled, as are*

*newspapers, cardboard and shredded white office paper; all kitchen waste goes through the composting system. An energy-saving programme ensures the fitting of energy-saving bulbs where appropriate and solar lights are used in the staff car parks"* (http://www.princeofwales.gov.uk/personalprofi les/residences/highgrove/).

In his book, "Highgrove: Portrait of an Estate" (1993), Charles described in loving care how little he knew at the time about gardening or environmentalism at the time of the Highgrove move: "It was difficult to know where to begin and I knew nothing about the practical aspects of gardening…" The quote of the book was telling for two reasons--it marks Charles first foray into environmental sensitivity, but more importantly, it marks where he started into the "practical" aspects of gardening as if to say he already knew about its potential political and economic aspects. Sometimes, there is more truth in what is *not* said, that in what is. What *is* critically important, and the key linking Charles with the darker aspects of Green politics, was that his mentor in the gardening and design at Highgrove, and most likely environmentalism in general, was Miriam Rothschild. The same Rothschild of the famed Rothschild power empire that handles substantial assets for many of the royal families of Europe.[45]

Miriam is an interesting member of the family, and well learned on the subject of environmental reform and environmentalism as a whole. A recognized expert in her field, she has written over 300 papers on the subject of environmental theory and zoology and holds honorary doctorates from Oxford and Cambridge. In 1997 she and Peter Marren co-authored "Rothschild's Reserves: Time and Fragile Nature," revisiting 182 nature reserves created by Charles Rothschild eighty-five years earlier to see what had become of them. She discovered that more than half had now been damaged or destroyed completely:

---

[45] Miriam Rothschild was born in 1908 in Ashton Wold, near Oundle in Northamptonshire, the daughter of Charles Rothschild of the Rothschild family of bankers and Rozsika Edle Rothschild (née von Wertheimstein), a Hungarian sportswoman. Her brother was Victor Rothschild, 3rd Baron Rothschild and one of her sisters (Kathleen Annie) Pannonica Rothschild (Baroness Nica de Koenigswarter) would later be a jazz enthusiast and patroness of Thelonious Monk and Charlie Parker.

*All my life I've had close connections with organizations* [sic] *in this country trying to conserve nature.... Conservation, farming and landscaping should be closely linked if we're going to succeed. When I was chairman of the local RSNC* [Royal Society for Nature Conservation], *I said that I'd only be chairman until we doubled our number of members, but that when we'd doubled it, I was going to leave. Everyone thought I'd be there for a long time, but within a year our numbers had doubled. For the first time in my life, I've seen a rise in consciousness in the population, although it's far too little, but it's going in the right direction."*

It is an almost certainty that Miriam, seeing the plight of her father's work, sought to repair the damage with her substantial influence on Prince Charles, and she is heavily credited with the development of the estate at Highgrove and perhaps even Charles' growing interest in environmentalism after his move there in 1980. The influence of Miriam Rothschild would not be out of character for the Rothschild family. They have been heavily involved with the Royals since the rise of Capitalism and America. The Rothschild's are a powerful family of bankers of European-German-Jewish decent, and are members of the Romanian baronies, the Hapsburgs. They were declared and validated as nobility by Queen Victoria, and their influence and wealth cannot be overstated. By some accounts the Rothschild's vast wealth may be the largest holdings of any individual family in the world. To say that the Rothschild's are the chief bankers and a major subsidizer of the Royals would be a fair assessment.

The Rothschild's link with the German and French governments during the period of Napoleonic domination through World War II is heavily documented. The family was in London in 1813 to 1815 and was instrumental in the financing of the British war effort. They financed the shipment of bullion to the Duke of Wellington's armies across Europe, and they arranged the payment of British financial subsidies to their Continental allies[46]. Nathan Rothschild's agents during the Napoleonic wars often supplied the English crown with information more accurately and well ahead of their own spy networks. This contributed to the family earning their nobility titles with full heredity rights[47].

Although there have been many ridiculous claims about the Rothschild's being part of an international conspiracy known as the "Illuminati" and that the family is an instigator of wars and instability to further their own ends, it cannot be denied that their enormous influence

---

[46] From 1809 Nathan Rothschild began to deal in gold bullion, and developed this as a cornerstone of his business. From 1811 on, in negotiation with Commissary-General John Charles Herries, he undertook to transfer money to pay Wellington's troops on his campaign in Portugal and Spain against Napoleon and later to make subsidy payments to British allies.

[47] In 1816, Nathan Rothschild, father of Miriam, had two elder brothers that were granted noble status (Baron) by the Emperor of Austria. They were now permitted to prefix the Rothschild name with von or de.

and knowledge of world events has led to their profits.[48] Rather than truly controlling world events, the Rothschild's are merely bankers who profit from the world political sphere. The family deals not only in currencies but also in information and guidance. That is not to say their actions did not directly or indirectly influence world politics--it most certainly did. But to say it did so in a deliberate manner, in a conspiratorial way, would be more than a moderate stretch of the truth.

The various claims to power called a "New World Order[49]" are also plentiful in modern literature as well as on various blogs and newscasts. Realist and objectivist thinking, however, would show otherwise. Many times

---

[48] "The Illuminati (plural of Latin illuminatus, "enlightened") is a name given to several groups, both historical and modern and both real and fictitious. Historically the name refers specifically to the Bavarian Illuminati, an Enlightenment-era secret society founded on May 1, 1776. In modern times it is also used to refer to a purported conspiratorial organization which acts as a shadowy "power behind the throne," allegedly controlling world affairs through present day governments and corporations, usually as a modern incarnation or continuation of the Bavarian Illuminati. In this context the Illuminati are believed to be the masterminds behind events that will lead to the establishment of a New World Order."- "Illuminati" Encyclopædia Britannica. 14 (11 ed.). NY: Encyclopædia Britannica, Inc.

[49] In conspiracy theory, the term New World Order refers to the emergence of a bureaucratic collectivist one-world government. Camp, Gregory S. (1997). Selling Fear: Conspiracy Theories and End-Times Paranoia.

when various people or leaders are involved in a common cause it can easily be misinterpreted as a conspiracy, but following that line of thought would lead to a clouding of the truth. The New World Order is merely a conglomeration of powerful people with similar interests (if it even exists at all); one that represents increasing the power of the elite over the holdings of independent minded people- not necessarily Royal in nature. Thus the actions and influence of Miriam Rothschild on Prince Charles is most likely not an act of political subterfuge but simply a matter of historical fact and being the person in the right place at the right time; a convenient matter of course, but nevertheless not for a nefarious purpose.

The Rothschild's bankrolling of the royal families and their influence is important to understanding the moves by the Royals in Green politics. Instead of some wild conspiracy theory, the Royals simply are using the Green Movement for their own ends--in essence "the enemy of my enemy is my friend." This is not to say that there is not a combined effort to bring down Capitalism and American business interests. On the contrary, these are the many ships that are sailing in a straight line on this matter. While there is no evidence that the various factions and representatives' of royal families and green political factions are *directly* conspiring against the American people, there is no doubt that an equal and unbending hatred of free capitalism exists in both. Shared common goals and a dislike of America is what is behind the Royals contacts and funding of green groups.

The most fascinating link to all of this, and thus the recent historical increase in influence of leftist theory in American politics, is that of a well known Hungarian who has been handling substantial amounts of Royal money for years, and recently began heavily bankrolling Progressive and Green politics in the United States.

His name is George Soros.[50]

---

[50] In 1973, Soros left Arnhold and S. Bleichroder to set up his own hedge fund with $12 million from investors. Christopher Ink was also involved and other partners have included Victor Niederhoffer and Stanley Druckenmiller, as well as a substantial investment from the Rothschild's family.

# Checkmate

*"You have the potential of a breakdown of the entire system if you have a slowdown of economic activity in the center even as inflationary pressures mount ... We're on the edge of it, yes."- George Soros*

Although the links to the royal families of Europe are obvious, with the Rothschild family as its financial nexus, the issue becomes more complex as it relates to American politics. With the evolution of the Royal's power base now involved more with money and the financial markets rather than in armies on the field, they have become doubly dangerous and far more effective than Kaiser Wilhelm could have ever imagined. George Soros, in acting as a worldwide banker of the Green and Progressive agenda, has had enormous influence on American political thought and the position of the American government. Part of that is due to his own personal dislike of George Bush, and part of it comes from his upbringing in Eastern Europe and his connections to the money and power of the Royals.

As a young man in his teens when Nazi Germany occupied Hungary, Soros worked for the Jewish Council, which had been established during the Nazi occupation of Hungary to forcibly carry out Nazi and Hungarian government anti-Jewish measures[51].

Soros, in a 1994 interview in the New Republic, described this time to writer Michael Lewis:

> *And there I was given these small slips of paper... It said report to the rabbi seminary at 9 a.m... And I was given this list of names. I took this piece of paper to my father. He instantly recognized it. This was a list of Hungarian Jewish lawyers. He said, 'You deliver the slips of paper and tell the people that if they report they will be deported... I'm not sure to what extent he knew they were going to be gassed. I did what my father said. There was one man I shall not forget. I took it to him and told him*

---

[51] During World War II, the Germans established Jewish councils, usually called Judenraete (sg., *Judenrat*). These Jewish municipal administrations were required to ensure that Nazi orders and regulations were implemented. Jewish council members also sought to provide basic community services for ghettoized Jewish populations. Forced to implement Nazi policy, the Jewish councils remain a controversial and delicate subject. Jewish council chairmen had to decide whether to comply or refuse to comply with German demands to, for example, listing the names of Jews for deportation- *US Holocaust Memorial Museum Encyclopedia*.

*what my father had said. He said: 'Tell your father that I am a law-abiding citizen, that I have always been a law-abiding citizen and I am not going to start breaking the law now.' And that stayed with me forever.*

During this period Soros lived with and posed as the godson of an employee of the Hungarian Ministry of Agriculture--a position that was often reserved for people of note such as members of Royal houses, an interesting early connection between Soros and some of the Royal lines. Soros also survived the Battle of Budapest in which Soviet and German forces fought house-to-house through the city. Soros immigrated to England in 1947 and lived with his uncle, an Orthodox Jew. His uncle paid his living expenses while he attended the London School of Economics where he received a Bachelor of Science in Philosophy in 1952. He eventually secured an entry-level position with the London merchant bank Singer & Friedlander. He has a cousin from that family era, Caron Enlander (née Weiss) in New York. By 1973 when investment regulations restricted his ability to run the funds as he wished, he resigned his position and

---

established a private investment company which evolved into the Quantum Fund. The Quantum Group of Funds are privately owned hedge funds based on the Curacao (Netherlands Antilles) and Cayman Islands. They are currently advised by George Soros through his company Soros Fund Management. The shareholders of the funds are not publicly disclosed although it is known that the Rothschild family and other wealthy Europeans put at least $6 million into the funds in 1969[52].

Soros also has a fairly extensive connection to the Royals through his familial ties. Business Insider reports that George Soros' nephew Peter Soros, a son of Paul Soros, is married to the former Flora Fraser—a daughter of Lady Antonia Fraser and the late Sir Hugh Fraser and a stepdaughter of the late 2005 Nobel Laureate Harold Pinter[53]. The connection to Lady Antonia Fraser is the most interesting of the royal familial connections to the Soros family. Fraser is the daughter of Frank Pakenham,

---

[52] Per the source Quantum Funds Online http://www.quantumfundsonline.us and *World's Champion Bull Rider* By FREDERICK UNGEHEUER/NEW YORK Time Magazine, 05/04/1987.

[53] "Peter Soros and Flora Fraser". New York Times (New York Times Company). February 2, 1997 in reference to Business Insider.

7th Earl of Longford (1905–2001) and his wife Elizabeth Pakenham, Countess of Longford, a.k.a. Elizabeth Harman (1906–2002). As the daughter of an Earl she is accorded the honorific courtesy title "Lady" and thus customarily addressed formally as "Lady Antonia[54]." Marriage of family, particularly heir apparent males, is the most common way non-nobility by birth family lines are bound to the nobility. This method was established by monarchies as early as the 1500's in order to insulate themselves from any possible risk of betrayal or damage. The Lady Antonia Fraser is a well established biographer of the Royals, and has done extensive work documenting the Royals' family trees and lines. She chronicled the life and times of Charles II in a well-reviewed 1979 eponymous biography.[55] The book was cited as an influence on the 2003 BBC/A&E mini-series, *Charles II: The Power & the Passion*. She has written several glorifying accounts of the Royals' history, including

---

[54] Mel Gussow, "The Lady Is a Writer", The New York Times Magazine, 9 Sept. 1984, Sunday Late City Final Ed., Sec. 6, Health: 60, col. 2. Print. New York Times, New York Times Company, 9 Sept. 1984, Web, 8 Apr. 2009.

[55] *King Charles II* (1979). Also published as *Royal Charles: Charles II and the Restoration and Charles II*. ISBN 075381403X.

works on The Gunpowder Plot, Louis X1V and Marie Antoinette.

Soros is no stranger to political intrigue or involving himself financially in the affairs of sovereign nations. Throughout his career he has invested substantial sums in "philanthropic" programs and movements; all of which have been significantly involved in dissident movements against both capitalistic and communist governments. He funded movements during the South African apartheid revolts for instance, as well as anti-government groups in communist iron curtain countries.

His substantial involvement with the Open Society Institute's [56] programs in Georgia were considered by Russian and Western observers to have been crucial in the success of the Rose Revolution.[57]

---

[56] A Soros foundation. From their website: "The Open Society Foundations work to build vibrant and tolerant democracies whose governments are accountable to their citizens. To achieve this mission, the Foundations seek to shape public policies that assure greater fairness in political, legal, and economic systems and safeguard fundamental rights." Of particular note from the website: "The Foundations place a high priority on protecting and improving the lives of people in marginalized communities." -www.soros.org/

[57] The "Revolution of Roses" (often translated into English as the Rose Revolution) was a change of power in Georgia in November 2003 which took place after widespread protests over the disputed parliamentary elections. As a result, President Eduard Shevardnadze was forced to resign on November 23, 2003.

Although Soros himself has said that his role in the Rose Revolution was "overstated," this is not the general consensus of outside sources.[58] The Rose Revolution ended the government of Eduard Shevardnadze who ran the Russian State of Georgia from 1995 to 2003 and was a protégé of Mikhail Gorbachev and was an institutor of many of Gorbachev's deconstructing policies in the old Soviet Union.

What was fascinating about the Rose Revolution was the symbolism of the opposition's forces who burst into the government's chambers carrying roses in hand to protest the Parliament session after the election. The War of the Roses from 1455 to 1485 was so named after the two "rose" factions of the House of Plantagenet (Lancaster and York) went to war with each other over control of the royal power in England. The victory in that war went to the "red rose" faction of Lancastrian Henry Tudor who then founded the House of Tudor by a marriage to Elizabeth of York, and thus ended the war. The House of Tudor ruled England for over 100 years

---

[58] Such as *Georgia: The Strange Silence of George Soros* by Mark Almond, or Robert Slater, *Soros. The Unauthorized Biography* (McGraw-Hill: New York, 1996).

125

and ended with Elizabeth I who died without an heir. The startling connection between the Lancastrian ancestry and the modern Royals is that the Lancaster inheritance, known as the Duchy of Lancaster, has remained in English and then British royal ownership continually since that period with monarchs bearing the title Duke of Lancaster. In 2007 the Duchy was valued at 397 million pounds, and the profits are the primary source of the current monarch's income[59].

Under Shevardnadze's pro-Western tenure, Georgia became a major recipient of United States foreign and military aid and signed a strategic partnership with NATO and declared an ambition to join both NATO and the European Union. Surely this did not sit well with the anti-capitalists of the Green Movement who were trying to increase their stranglehold on NATO in Europe. If the former Soviet satellite nations were doing business with the West and eventually joined NATO, access to their resources would undermine everything that the Green Movement was trying to accomplish. The securing of a $3 billion project to build pipelines carrying oil from

---

[59] Web archive of the Duchy of Lancaster official report, page 48.

Azerbaijan to Turkey via Georgia assured that NATO would have an almost limitless amount of oil on tap. Thus Soros' involvement in the Rose Revolution undermined the very energy reserves that NATO needed to maintain a strong footprint in Europe. There were also parallels between the fall of a pro-Western Georgia to the Yugoslav revolution in 2000 where Yugoslav President Slobodan Milosevic was also forced to resign by mass protests funded by the Soros financial machine. It was the Open Society Institute of George Soros once again which arranged contacts between the Georgian opposition and the Yugoslav Otpor! movement[60], which had been instrumental in the toppling of Milosevic[61]. Otpor! activists reportedly advised the Georgian opposition on the methods that they had used to mobilize popular anger against Milosevic. According to the then editor-in-chief of The Georgian Messenger newspaper, Zaza Gachechiladze in 2003: "It's generally accepted public

---

[60] Otpor! was a non-partisan civic youth movement in Serbia that employed nonviolent struggle as their course of action. They were credited for their role in the successful overthrow of Slobodan Milosevic in October 2000.

[61] Georgia Revolt Carried Mark of Soros: Mark Mackinnon From Wednesday's Globe and Mail, November 26, 2003.

opinion here that Mr. Soros is the person who planned Shevardnadze's overthrow."

The Institute for War and Peace Reporting wrote in an interview held with the press at his home that Shevardnadze "spoke with anger" about a plot by "unspecified Western figures" to bring him down. When pressed on the subject during the interview he declined to answer, but specifically said it was not coming from the United States administration. Members of the Otpor! movement in Yugoslavia, have also been active in Egypt, Tunisia, Libya, Azerbaijan, Tonga, Burma and Zimbabwe as well as labor, anti-war and immigration rights activists in the United States[62].

Although the new Saakashvili government of Georgia is still decidedly pro-Western and pro-NATO, some questions have arisen from Georgia's business dealings and internal corruption following voter fraud issues in 2008. The relationship between Saakashvili and the West still remains a large question mark, and he has been described as precarious and volatile[63]. In the 2010

---

[62] Serbia: 10 Years Later: The Huffington Post, June 17, 2009.

[63] *U.S. Ally Proves Volatile Amid Dispute With Russia-* Marc Champion, Wall Street Journal 9/30/2008.

study *Competitive Authoritarianism: Hybrid Regimes After the Cold War*, political scientists Steven Levitsky and Lucan A. Way cite various media and human rights reports to describe Saakashvili's Georgia as "competitive authoritarian"--a shortened description of a government that on the surface seems democratic and free and is an essentially non-democratic state run by a dictatorial government under the guise of a puppet Parliament. The current government of Georgia thus is, in effect, a feudalistic endeavor, and a virtual prototype for the Royal's future plans for other countries where the illusion of freedom keeps the people happy while control of resources and power remains in the hands of a select few. Furthermore, the previous model of the 2000 Yugoslav revolution, has led to today's Serbia being an autocratically controlled democracy where Progressive politics have gradually encroached on traditional free market capitalism.

This prototype of an authoritarian democracy is essential to understanding the moves in other countries, particularly the United States. A move toward a socialistic government like in Germany and England was not to be reasonably expected even under the best of circumstances in America. Thus power would have to be consolidated in fewer hands while still maintaining the illusion of a free government, albeit a government that would dictate the lifestyle of the individuals living under it as well as control the resources and major branches of free enterprise. The Yugoslav model of conversion of capitalism to Progressive control, and the Rose Revolution in Russian Georgia are the previous examples of this.

In the past 20 years American politics has been mainly dominated by a handful of individuals, most notably the Bush family of Texas and the Clinton factional camp of the moderate left. However, with the ascendency of Barack Obama into the White House, American politics has taken a decidedly left turn from the more moderate Clinton wing of the Democratic Party. Obama's politics are most certainly further left than the majority of the American electorate, and Green political interests have played a large role in his election and rise to power.

The ascendency of Obama into the White House was no easy task, and was certainly unexpected by the Clintons who clearly were caught relatively unaware of his sudden rise in popularity. Whether Obama's personal viewpoint was further left of the Clinton's is hard to say, but he certainly was more willing to implement far leftist and Green politics more radically than his Arkansas competitor. While the power base and political thought of the Clintons is no doubt left of center, it is substantially funded by the free enterprise capitalists of American business. The Clintons also have extensive relationships with many American business interests, and during Bill Clinton's Presidency he promoted many pro-business governmental changes, most notably the de-regulation of the banking and investment houses.[64] This deregulation led to a massive expansion of the financial sector, and the wealth generated by this expansion was both substantial and widespread. The expansion of the American economy under Bill Clinton rivaled that of Ronald Reagan's tenure and assured profound funding for numerous social welfare projects. Obama's rise was long

---

[64] The Gramm–Leach–Bliley Act, a.k.a the Financial Services Modernization Act of 1999, was signed into law by President Bill Clinton and it essentially repealed the Glass–Steagall Act of 1933, opening up the market among banking companies, securities companies and insurance companies. The Glass–Steagall Act previously had prohibited any one institution from acting as any combination of an investment bank, a commercial bank, and an insurance company.

in the making and began not in 2007 with the beginning of his campaign but back in 2004 and 2005 with the move of the House and Senate into Democrat controlled hands, and thus the foundation to build a Progressive and Green presidency. There could have been no Barrack Obama in the White House without a Nancy Pelosi in the House or the powerful green funded Harry Reid in the Senate. The shift in the control in Congress actually provided more substance and strength to the Green Movement in American politics than the achievement of capturing the White House. This shift in Congressional power was heavily funded by George Soros in the late 1990's and thus by default, the Royal houses of Europe due to the large deposits of cash with the Quantum Fund.

Green politics had been in complete disarray with the collapse of the Carter administration and his failure to turn around an abysmal economy in the late 1970's. Green politics, solar energy and oil efficiency were the buzzwords of that period as well (mirroring the rise of the Greens in Germany at the time), and had the same results on the American economy in 1976 as it is having now in 2010. The American people's frustration with Carter and his economic policies culminated in the election of

Ronald Reagan in 1980, and the fiscal domination of the Republican Party for nearly 25 years. People were not quick to forget the long gas lines, the expensive cost of living increases and the failed foreign policies of the Carter administration. After America elected Clinton in 1993, he was hard pressed to take America back toward Progressivism and a controlled economy. After just 2 years in office Clinton was forced to make compromise after compromise with a Republican Congress in order to maintain his Presidency.

The Green Party, and the Progressives that backed them, believed the real limitation to Clinton's success during his Presidency was not his lack of enthusiasm for leftist politics but rather his inability to legislate past the obstacle of a Republican controlled Congress. The American left learned from that experience. This time around they would establish a firm control on Congress first and capture the White House last thus ensuring at least two years of pure political power to press the progressive agenda on an unwilling American people.

When President Obama was elected to office his radical agenda of Progressivism was hurried through legislation at almost breakneck speed. He understood that he would never be as powerful as he was in January of 2009, and without the considerable political capital he was about to expend, the progressive agenda and the green political machine would eventually run out of gas much as it did on Bill Clinton in his first administration.

Congressional seats are far more easily manipulated and purchased through the infusion of cash and political activism, than the White House or the presidency. Because of its segmented nature, Congress is more vulnerable to local politics, heavy advertising and the "ground game" of door knocking and petition signing. The real trick would be the White House. The Bush administration fighting wars on two fronts and faced with the threat of a hostile terrorist enemy banging on the American gates would be virtually impossible to unseat. Proof of that existed in 2004 when Bush defeated Kerry in a relatively close election, despite the unpopularity of wars in the Mideast, growing long-term problems in the economy and a number of scandalous incidents which cast the party in a bad light.

The opportunity came in 2008 when no clear leadership came from the Republican Party that faced a potentially deep recession and failures in Iraq and

Afghanistan. Most damaging of all was the failure of the ability of Bush administration to capture Bin Laden and the ultimate collapse of the real estate bubble which had been building for years.

The problem, as it lay at the feet of the political left and Green politicians, was Hilary Clinton. Hilary had no intention of potentially shipwrecking her administration on the issues of the far left such as health care and government oversight and control of the economy. Hilary just would not play ball. She supported the successful strategy in Iraq and had taken more moderate opinions and positions as the "Senator from New York." She was clearly preparing for a massive run at the White House, and the Clinton train was nigh unstoppable once it got rolling. She had planned for the 2008 election to be a coronation not a trench fight for the minds of the Democratic party. Although Barack Obama had become a rival as early as 2006, he was not gaining the momentum needed to capture the Presidency and did not seem to appeal to much of middle America as the more moderate Hilary Clinton.

The key again was the old Rothschild money invested with George Soros after the fall of Carter, and his subtle purchasing of the Clinton machine behind Hilary's back. "If you can't beat 'em, buy 'em." This was the mantra of the Green Party, and backed with the enormous wealth of the Soros' people and the Royals it became critical to Obama's success.

Late in 2004 Soros quietly began funding various leftist groups that traditionally had been Clinton territory. He funded MoveOn.org, a strong left wing proponent, and the website took on an even more strident position on American politics. [65]His influence spread to various media outlets and newspapers as his holding companies and investment houses made significant but selective purchases. His connections with General Electric (which owned NBC at the time) and MSNBC run deep, mainly stemming from his involvement with Air America radio, which ultimately failed. Air America's commentator Rachel Maddow ended up in a key position at MSNBC,

---

[65] According to an article in the Washington Post dated March 10, 2004- "The Democratic 527 organizations have drawn support from some wealthy liberals determined to defeat Bush. They include financier George Soros who gave $1.46 million to MoveOn.org Voter Fund (in the form of matching funds to recruit additional small donors); Peter B. Lewis, chief executive of the Progressive Corp., who gave $500,000 to MoveOn.org Voter Fund; and Linda Pritzker, of the Hyatt hotel family, and her Sustainable World Corp., who gave $4 million to the joint fundraising committee."

and former Air America celebrity, Saturday Night Live's own Al Franken even ended up getting a seat in Congress in Minnesota.

Thus with a strong influence on American media and newspapers, the bomb was dropped on Hillary Clinton midway through her campaign when, shortly before the Iowa caucuses, Oprah Winfrey announced she would support Barack Obama rather than Clinton in the 2008 election. Oprah had an enormous amount of influence on middle America. Her Oprah book club was practically a built in multi-million vote getter.

Before the middle of the 2008 American presidential election and up until the Oprah endorsement, the Clintons always considered the African-American vote as a considerable power base for their operations. Oprah's support of Obama effectively ended that cooperation between African-American voters and the Clinton camp. Obama would now be seen as an essentially colorblind hero of the left, and with the media exposure the Soros' machine could provide him, he would be a formidable opponent. It was an endorsement that carried substantial weight, but Clinton did not see the freight train coming at her. Endorsement after endorsement of former Clintonites soon fell in place after the Oprah endorsement. Even Hollywood fell in love with the visually appealing Obama. He was attractive, young and idealistic which always has appealed to the American left. The Soros media machine painted Clinton as strident and hostile, and tied her to the more unsavory elements of her husband's Presidency.

Soros and the Greens did not win the White House in 2008, they won it in 2006 with the Democratic victories in Congress, and no one had bothered to tell Hilary Clinton. Although the primary was contentious (no one could campaign like the Clintons), in the end it was a hopeless task as the well compensated media continued to cast aside the many warning flags of Obama's extreme progressive brand of Liberalism and provided picture after picture of the hapless Hilary Clinton in various argumentative pictures, shots and videos; subtlety painting her as a left-wing version of John McCain--angry and unelectable.

Thus with Barack Obama firmly in the White House, and the Congress established as a left-wing supermajority, the green political machine put a full court press of their agenda onto the American people. They did so with ferocious speed and commitment knowing full well that the net effect of their policies would bankrupt the American economy and as a result would cause a massive backlash by the American voters in the election of 2010, much as it had done with Carter. Obama would never be as powerful as he would be upon taking the oath office, and they wasted not a minute of time moving in on the economy.

In as short as a few hours after Obama's inauguration, he issued more executive orders than George Bush did in the last four years of his presidency. Consolidating power quickly he used the spreading recessionary wildfire as a tool to pay off political favors and debts and establish his authority over the revamped Democrat Party as, not only a party of the far left, but as the party that would finally establish the Green Movement as America's dominate political theory. This consolidation of power in the hands of a few White House autocrats was similar to that seen in the Georgian Rose Revolution in 2003, including the appointing of various "czars" as both political payoffs and power consolidating moves.

Companies like General Electric (GE) who had an important role in green politics would receive vast amounts of money from the new Troubled Asset Relief Program (TARP) which was originally designed to protect banks from imploding in the collapse in the real estate market. GE made the case that since it has large amounts of exposure in the insurance industry it could tap TARP monies for their own use. The argument was thin, but it nevertheless stuck as an all too eager leftist Congress played ball with their new team captain. The media spin machine went into overdrive with the Obama agenda and how it would save America from the evils of Capitalism, and ignore over 300 years of economic success for what was originally a rather minor crisis in the real estate industry.

Had the real estate crisis of 2008-2009 been handled as the savings and loan crisis was handled in 1991-1992, by simply buying up the toxic assets and redistributing them at bargain prices, the issue of economic recovery would have been a minor one. As it stood, the sweeping regulatory changes and seizure of private industries by the American government exacerbated the growing recession and in doing so emptied the government coffers. The massive regulatory expansion of 2009 and 2010 and the enormous push for green political favors at the expense of American businesses forced them to retreat from the borrowing they were used to and cut payrolls drastically. The result was a massive explosion of the unemployment rate to over 10% within 10 months of Obama's rise to power.

All of this was intended from the start. America was now essentially bankrupt and in debt to its bondholders and could no longer play power politics in a worldwide economy. It would be forced to retreat from its considerable military and financial interests in the Mideast which threatened the emergence of the royal families return to economic power. Without sizeable economic gratuities from the American government, small countries dependent on American foreign aid could not meet obligations. Economies worldwide began to suffer. Food prices rose as a result of American monetary policy, and the long term effects of corn price increases because of its green use as an ethanol substitute for gasoline. Unrest swelled worldwide as inflation began to spiral upward in 2010 and subsidies of American aid became less valuable.

The stranglehold on the American economy by its own government was the checkmate move by the Royals, as they now could begin to advance their final agenda in Europe and break the view that Capitalism was the solution to the world's problems. The economic upheavals in Europe that resulted in the collapse of the PIGS'[66] economies could never had even been imagined much less attempted with a healthy American economy. As it stood, the European economies fell like dominoes as America stood by and watched, turning her back on its once close allies of Israel and Egypt. The moves by Islamacists in the Mediterranean and the Mideast were the direct result of the American economic collapse, the increase in food prices and inflation of the dollar. Extremist Jihadists and moderate Muslims alike were now being positioned as enemies to America fueled by dried up entitlements of American supported dictatorships.

The profits rolled in as the Royals had positioned themselves in gold and commodities years prior in

---

[66] PIGS is a grouping acronym used by analysts, academics and by the international press, that refers to the faltering economies of Portugal, Italy, Greece, and Spain.

preparation for recessionary collapse, and the former enemies of monarchical power were now powerless to stop them.

# So Now What?

*Change will not come if we wait for some other person or some other time. We are the ones we've been waiting for. We are the change that we seek. - Barack Obama*

What the Royal families' plan to do with the newfound buckets of power and money is anyone's guess at this point. Revenge on the American electorate and way of life was certainly a priority but probably was not the total end goal of green politics and Progressivism. The game is never truly over with the Royals, and it is hard to imagine an actual rise to direct governance again by kings and queens. It is always possible the Royals will simply now use their bulwarked position to direct countries and populations to their own ends much as they did before the American Revolution of 1776. In short, they have and will establish a feudalistic control over economies and the people that live in them.

Their hold on power, by the nature of a lack of direct authority, makes it tenuous for them to use too heavy a hand. Anything is possible of course, and Prince

Charles' son William is now due for marriage, children and possible ascendency to the throne of England. With his claim of familial right on the throne both by blood and now political influence and wealth, expect to see him influence the Queen to commit to an abdication, even if her hold on the throne has rivaled that of Victoria.

In Germany the royal heir George Freidrich Ferdninand has made a few headlines by talking publicly about a return to direct royal authority and governance. Such talk would have been unheard of 20 years ago, but passed now with nary a word from straighter thinking individuals or the German government. Crown Princess Victoria of Sweden has not spoken of it publicly, but in June 2010 she married a commoner Daniel Westling thus establishing her legal claim to the throne under the terms of the Swedish Act of Succession. Frederik, The Crown Prince of Denmark, published his book on green theory in 2010, *Naturen og klimaændringerne i Nordøstgrønland* (The Nature and Climate Change in Greenland).

The last of the French Bourbons, Louis Alphonse, has found a home in the leftist Venezuela and makes his claims to the now defunct French throne. From there he works for the Chavez controlled Bank of Venezuela. An important point is that his wife, a Venezuelan heiress named Mary Marguerite, had their first child, a daughter named Eugénie on March 5, 2007 at the Mount Sinai Medical Center in Miami, Florida--thus technically making her a natural born American citizen. She was baptized at the papal nunciature in Paris in June 2007 and legitimists recognize her as Princess Eugénie of Bourbon. In 2010 the couple also flew Marguerite to New York to have their twin boys, although they too were christened in Europe. The Vatican itself performed the ceremony.

They are also not the only Royals which have endeavored to make sure their children were born on American soil, a fact that has gone largely unnoticed by the American media. The implications of this may be varied and complex, but no evidence exists that anything nefarious may be afoot on this issue. Still it is one that bears watching, since most rules of accession do not specifically state that a person or persons must be born in their county of rule. For example, the current King of Thailand was born in the United States[67].

---

[67] Bhumibol was born at the Mount Auburn Hospital in Cambridge, Massachusetts, in the United States on 12/05/1927.

If the Royals recognize one thing, they know how unrest is generated and how hard it is to quell once it achieves critical mass. The activity of populations against their thrones at the turn of the 18<sup>th</sup> century and again in the mid-1800's revolved around a central shortage of food. This factors into recent movements by the Greens toward less productive methods of organic farming and corn shortages rising from the diverting of corn crops to make biofuels instead of feed and food products.

The availability of food has increased geometrically with the advent of modern farming techniques and the agricultural advances of the 20<sup>th</sup> century. As a result, the world (up until only very recently) is essentially in its most stable period since the Pax Romana period of the Roman empire.[68] When people are well fed and well entertained they are far less likely to revolt against their leaders no matter how bad other conditions may be. Few intelligent individuals, who have a family to feed would risk losing the basic necessities of

---

[68] Pax Romana (Latin for "Roman peace") was the long period of relative peace and minimal expansion by military forces experienced by the Roman Empire in the 1st and 2nd centuries AD. Since it was established by Caesar Augustus it is sometimes called Pax Augusta. Its span was approximately 207 years.

life over a set of principles on the finer points of constitutional government. If people have jobs to go to and food on the table, they are far less likely to pick up a torch and march on the castle. Thus today's society is unlikely to cast aside Capitalism and Democracy in exchange for a planned society or revert back to direct monarchical rule. Unless, of course, the world food supply is threatened.

While science fiction novels and comic books talk about governments or enemies poisoning the food and water supplies in order to create mayhem, the practical realities of such a feat are implausible. Nevertheless, such a feat would absolutely be required in order to create enough unrest for a population to ignore the success of 250 plus years of profitable capitalism. So how do you skin the cat? A start is to destabilize the currency so badly that the actual COST of food goes through the roof. When a shortage is created it is virtually impossible even for the wealthiest individuals to feed themselves.

From 2007 to 2010 the Federal Reserve embarked on a policy of managed currency by purchasing and then reselling large amounts of United States treasury bonds in order to generate capital to fund their expansion of government. This policy, better known as "quantitative easing" or QE2 ("Two" for the fact this is the second time it was done, the first time being under Obama in 2008)[69] would increase the overall value of the United States treasury in exchange for devaluing the United States currency. Most economic experts agree that such devaluation would cause a large increase in inflation and as a result food prices[70]. The current United States administration's attitude toward inflation is at best a low risk due to the deflationary effects of the recession, and the they are setting United States monetary policy accordingly. With the value of the dollar decimated by inflationary pressures, the natural effects of a shortage of food would be much more severe.

The food shortage fits neatly into the move of corn products into the ethanol market. Corn exports for the use of greener ethanol fuel; have increased by more than 100 fold since 2007, and now 25% of United States'

---

[69] QE2 is short for a second round of so-called quantitative easing, announced by the Fed in November 2010, that would have the Fed by $600 billion in U.S. Treasuries in order to lower long-term interest rates and drive an economic recovery.

[70] For example Phillip Cagan, The Monetary Dynamics of Hyperinflation, in Milton Friedman (Editor), *Studies in the Quantity Theory of Money*, Chicago: University of Chicago Press (1956).

corn production is being diverted for biofuels[71]. As a result, the availability of corn for food production and land for growing other food crops is at a premium. According to the United States Department of Agriculture, in 2010 food prices were growing upward at a rate twice the inflation rate--an inflation rate that will soon explode from the Federal Reserve's QE2 policy.

This puts an especially hard economic pressure on poor countries that rely on cheap United States food exports and subsidized pricing. The United States is the primary supplier of world food exports, particularly to third world or impoverished nations such as Tunisia, Egypt and many other African nations. These nations are now facing crushing debt, and food shortages, along with the world-wide recession from the collapse of the American real estate market and the shift of money to the gold market. This creates an environment that is ripe for toppling governments by populist movements such as Communism, Socialism and religious extremist oligarchies.

---

[71] The Potential Impacts of Increased Corn Production for Ethanol, G.Lakes, 2007.

The expression "let them eat cake" has now been turned on its head from the Royals to the corporate Capitalists whose policies have fed the world for centuries. It is an ironic twist that the very shortages that were used against the French crown in 1790 are being recycled into a modern day equivalent. The United States farms provide far more food than the world could ever eat and yet populations are starving because the pricing of the food is beyond the reach of poorer nations, even at rock bottom prices. The ingenuity of the Royals in their manipulation of currency and commodity pricing is complex and clear--destabilize the currency markets so that the wealth built up over the last 200 years is now worthless, and let their hunger drive their demand for governmental change. Naturally the Royals would gain the benefit of that change as they had properly laid the groundwork for their rise again to power.

Recent events in Egypt, Tunisia and Jordan are all a direct or indirect result of the world recessionary problem and food shortages directly due to America's current economic policies and exacerbated by green politics putting enormous pressures on currencies and feed pricing. A reformation of a new Islamic empire, ala the Ottoman empire of the 1300's, would be catastrophic to Western economies primarily due to our dependence on foreign oil. A unified Arab superpower would have an economic stranglehold on Western power which, if left unchecked, could result in another world war as the former superpowers of the West struggled for energy supremacy. The Royals of Europe's return to supremacy after a decimated population would then be indeed possible.

There is already talk of how a post-apocalyptic world would be much better off than it is currently. Articles abound in scientific journals regarding how a small nuclear confrontation would offset the damage from global warming--a frightening thought indeed[72]. A desperate population with collapsed legal and societal protections might seek help from returning to power a benevolent monarchical dictatorship; perhaps one where the people have some sort of illusionary democratic freedoms similar to that established in Russian Georgia.

---

[72] A recent NASA study delved into a horrible subject; that somehow a limited nuclear war would be "beneficial" to the environment by counteracting the effects of global warming. National Geographic, February, 2011.

The Progressive Movement has long held in its tenets that human beings are currently overpopulating the planet, and human overpopulation is an obstacle to a greener earth. What better way to reduce the populations and make them more dependent on government than a limited nuclear war where large cities were wiped out and huge tracts of land are left unusable from fallout? Not a large scale conflict mind you, but a smaller more "manageable" conflict. President Obama has already attempted to begin the process to control the manufacture and spread of large nuclear scale weapons in both the United States and Russia but has done little if nothing to halt the spread of smaller-scaled nuclear weapons or to prevent the spread of nuclear weapons to nations hostile to America (such as Iran or North Korea). In the book *Excessive Force Power Politics and Population Control*, 1996, Elizabeth Liagin discusses the problem of human overpopulation and suggests that the involvement of branches of the U.S. government are elevating population control to a top priority for the West.

Certainly the era of sparkling prosperity under free ownership of land, resources and businesses would be over in populations controlled by government planning, much as they are in China. But by then the argument would be simple to make that such capitalistic endeavors had led to a third world war (this time possibly nuclear) and subsequent massive economic collapse. History is written by the victors not by those cast aside, and it would be an easy task under a feudalistic type of government where media and speech are controlled and disseminated by government to make this argument.

However, the massive machine of the Royals and the powers that align themselves with them can be undone. Like most denizens of the underworld, the simple act of shining a light on their activities is often enough to halt their spread. Only through exposure and a public awareness of the forces behind the impending storm can it be stopped.

# ABOUT THE AUTHOR

Thomas Purcell lives in Glendale, AZ. He was born in Yonkers, NY, and at the age of four was the youngest member of Mensa. To date he is the highest tested individual in Mensa at that age. Educated at the University of California Tom moved to Arizona after college in 1994 and went into the insurance business. In 2005 after being a top agent for NY Life Insurance, he decided to become an independent broker (Lotusbenefits.com) and is now a successful entrepreneur and author of the column "Conservative Issues from the Desert." In Arizona he does volunteer work for conservative issues around the state. Objective, funny and a candidly frank speaker, Tom is available for consultation and speaking engagements on subjects from politics to marketing. You can read more of his musings and articles at www.thomas-purcell.com, as well as excerpts from his books, where he welcomes comments, discussion and offers free subscriptions.

www.ingramcontent.com/pod-product-compliance
Lightning Source LLC
Chambersburg PA
CBHW061300280526
45784CB00002B/831